For my Dad, Ken

Let's eat!

100+ favourites
Mostly healthy, always delicious

Nadia Lim

NUDE
FOOD

Contents

HELLO!

Welcome to *Let's eat*! I hope you will share and enjoy countless meals with your family and friends from the earmarked, splattered, and eventually tattered, pages of this book. The recipes in here are favourites that we cook and eat at home again and again, whether it's just myself, Carlos and Bodhi, or we have family or friends over for a relaxed gathering or a more special occasion.

In the last couple of years, life has brought some welcome changes with becoming a family of three and spending more time at home. It has meant there have been a few little changes to the way we eat. We have dinner much earlier for a start (I always wondered how anyone could have dinner at 5pm, now I know!), more child-friendly meals, more date nights at our 'home restaurant', and more family and friends visiting. I've enjoyed these changes and how it reflects in the way we eat. It has taken me 'back home', to when I was growing up and the recipes and meals I loved as a child.

My last few cookbooks have generally been written with a specific aim in mind, whether weight loss or complete dinner meals. My aim for this book was simply to include what we love eating. So there's a wide variety of dishes in here, most with fond memories attached, whether it's my (Malaysian) Dad's favourite Nasi Lemak (slightly altered for Kiwi tastebuds), the Chocolate Crème Brûlée that helped win Carlos' heart for good, or Bodhi's first-birthday Watermelon 'Cake'. I've also given recipes for things we eat all the time, such as my Everyday Green Smoothie and Turmeric and Ginger Chicken Soup (for when one of us is in need of some TLC) and revisited some of my childhood favourites, which I've put a fresher, more delicious twist on, such as Cauliflower Cheese Fettucine, Chocolate and Raspberry Lamingtons, Bountiful Bars (a-ma-zing!) and Jelly-tipped Ice-creams!

There's no doubt that home-cooked food makes us happier and healthier. It means we're eating more real food, or 'nude food' as I like to call it. Nutrition will always be an important part of my recipes and, quite simply, food with lots of brilliant fresh produce and more nourishing ingredients just tastes better anyway. However, I am also a believer of having all things in moderation (including moderation sometimes), so you'll see I've also included my top-ten treat recipes for special occasions. Eat well 90 percent of the time, and have whatever you want the other 10 percent of the time is my motto!

I hope you end up loving these recipes and cooking them as much as our family does, and that you'll have some great memories of eating them around the table with your loved ones.

Happy cooking and eating!

Nadia

Nadia Lim

BREAKFAST

SOME OF OUR WEEKDAY AND WEEKEND FAVOURITES TO GET EVERYONE OFF TO A GOOD START

Good morning!

+ BRUNCH

Pumpkin pie pancakes with apple and walnuts

SERVES 4 **PREP TIME** 15 minutes
COOK TIME 20 minutes (+ 40 minutes to pre-cook pumpkin)

DF (use DF milk + coconut oil) **| GF** (use mix of buckwheat + GF flour)

PANCAKES
pumpkin (or butternut), roasted and mashed, ¾ cup (see Note page 12)
banana (ripe) 1 large
free-range eggs 3
milk 1 cup
vanilla essence or extract 1 teaspoon
salt pinch of
brown sugar 2 tablespoons
self-raising flour 1 cup (or a mix of buckwheat and GF flour + 1 teaspoon baking powder)
baking powder 1 teaspoon
ground ginger ¼ teaspoon
mixed spice ½ teaspoon
ground cinnamon 1 teaspoon
ground nutmeg ½ teaspoon
coconut oil or butter to cook

APPLE AND WALNUTS
walnuts ¼ cup, chopped (optional)
coconut oil or butter 1 tablespoon
apples 3, peeled and diced
ground cinnamon ¼ teaspoon
brown sugar 2 teaspoons

TO SERVE
yoghurt (dairy or coconut)
maple syrup

I ate these in a café once and thought the inclusion of pumpkin was genius; I had to try recreating the recipe as soon as I got home. These are light and fluffy, with the perfect amount of warming spice. I've thrown a banana in the mixture for extra sweetness, which also results in the edges of the pancakes becoming a little caramelised and crispy as they cook.

1 Preheat oven to 50°C . Place pumpkin, banana, eggs, milk, vanilla, salt and sugar in a blender and blend until smooth and there are no lumps.

2 Sift flour, baking powder and spices into a large mixing bowl. Make a well in the centre and pour in pumpkin mixture. Whisk together until a smooth, uniform batter forms.

3 Heat about 2 teaspoons of coconut oil or butter in a large non-stick fry pan on medium heat. Pour half ladleful of pancake batter into the fry pan. Cook for about 2 minutes on one side until little bubbles start to appear on the surface, then carefully flip with a fish slice and cook for about 2 minutes on the other side, or until pancakes are golden brown and just cooked through. You should be able to cook about three at a time. Keep pancakes warm on a plate in the oven while you cook the remaining batter.

continued over page...

4 Once you have cooked all the pancakes, wipe out fry pan with paper towels. Place walnuts in the fry pan and toast on medium heat for a few minutes, tossing frequently to avoid burning. Set aside. Melt coconut oil or butter in the fry pan. Add apples and cinnamon and cook for a few minutes, then add sugar and walnuts, and toss to coat and caramelise.

5 To serve, stack a few pancakes on each plate and top with Apple and Walnuts. Serve with yoghurt and a drizzle of maple syrup.

To cook pumpkin or butternut, toss 600–700g (peeled and chopped) with a drizzle of oil and maple syrup on an oven tray lined with baking paper. Roast at 180°C for 40–45 minutes or until soft and slightly caramelised.

ENERGY	CARBS	PROTEIN	FAT	SAT FAT	SUGARS
1878kj / 449kcal	62.5g	15.1g	13.7g	5.3g	35.6g

Honey and balsamic roasted strawberries and rhubarb

SERVES 4 **PREP TIME** 5 minutes **COOK TIME** 20–25 minutes   **DF | GF**

Super simple, but super delish with sweet and tangy flavours. This is great for breakfast with your muesli and yoghurt, but equally good for a simple but stunning dessert with ice-cream.

rhubarb 1 bunch (about 400g or 6 long stalks)
strawberries (ripe) 1 large punnet (300–500g), hulled and any larger ones cut in half
orange zest and juice of 1
vanilla essence or extract 1 teaspoon
cinnamon sticks 1–2
honey 3 tablespoons
balsamic vinegar 2–3 teaspoons

Storage
Will keep in the fridge for up to one week.

1 Preheat oven to 180°C. Trim and cut rhubarb into 6cm-long pieces (if any pieces of rhubarb are especially wider than the rest, halve lengthways).

2 Place rhubarb in a large baking dish, along with strawberries and cinnamon stick(s). Scatter with orange zest, juice and vanilla. Drizzle with honey and balsamic vinegar. Bake for about 20–25 minutes until rhubarb is just tender (test with the tip of a knife) but still holding its shape. Spoon the juices over the fruit a few times during cooking.

3 Serve warm, at room temperature or cold with yoghurt and muesli … or for dessert, with ice-cream!

ENERGY	CARBS	PROTEIN	FAT	SAT FAT	SUGARS
451kj / 108kcal	21.6g	1.6g	0.6g	0g	21.3g

My everyday green smoothie

spinach, baby spinach or kale leaves
1 big handful, chopped (if using kale discard the tough stalks)
oranges 2, skin cut off (remove seeds)
lemon 1, skin cut off (remove seeds)
fresh turmeric 2–3cm piece, peeled and chopped (optional)
fresh ginger 2–3cm piece, peeled and chopped
cold water 1 cup
ice cubes 4–5

Tips

• Add ½ avocado to the mix if you'd like a creamy green smoothie.
• Add ½–1 cup chopped pineapple (without the core), or mango to the mix if you'd like a sweeter smoothie, or if you're a first-time green smoothie drinker.
• Add a peeled ripe kiwifruit for an extra vitamin C boost.
• Add a small handful of flat-leaf parsley, mint or basil for an extra nutrient boost and a subtle herby flavour.

This is our green smoothie that we have almost every morning with breakfast. Even Bodhi loves it! It's full of goodness with loads of vitamin C, folate, fibre and other vitamins and minerals. It's an understatement to say that it's a great way to start the day!

1 Place all ingredients in a blender, put the lid on tightly (as it will splash!) and blitz until smooth. Depending on how powerful your blender is, you might need to blitz it for more/less time to ensure that there are no stringy green bits left.

2 Pour into glasses, drink and feel good!

ENERGY	CARBS	PROTEIN	FAT	SAT FAT	SUGARS
281kj / 67kcal	11.9g	1.8g	0.5g	0.1g	11.7g

Raspberry chia jam

MAKES 1 x 300ml jar **PREP TIME** 5 minutes   DF I GF

frozen raspberries (defrosted) 2 cups
chia seeds 3 tablespoons
vanilla essence or extract ½ teaspoon
sugar (or liquid honey or maple syrup)
2–3 tablespoons, to taste

I never thought there could be such a thing as a healthy jam, but here you go! By using chia seeds you get a jammy jelly texture that usually needs loads of sugar to achieve. Believe it or not, this jam only has a couple of tablespoons of sweetener (not a whole cup like most jam recipes!). You can do so much more with it than have it on toast: it makes a delicious fruity topping for muesli or yoghurt, custard or ice-cream. I've even used it in my Baby Coconut Sponge Lamingtons (page 174) and Jam 'n Cream Coconut Flour Sponge Sandwich (page 160).

1 Place all ingredients in a blender and blitz until well combined.

2 Sweeten to taste with a little more sugar or honey, if needed.

3 Store in a clean bowl or jar in the fridge. The chia seeds will swell, creating a thick, jammy texture after a couple of hours.

Storage

Will keep in the fridge
for up to one week.

ENERGY	CARBS	PROTEIN	FAT	SAT FAT	SUGARS
182kj / 43kcal	6.2g	11.1g	1.6g	0.2g	4.2g

(per serving, 2 tablespoons)

Creamy herby baked eggs

SERVES 1, but you can increase this recipe to make as many as you like
PREP TIME 5 minutes **COOK TIME** 15–20 minutes

PER PERSON
butter a little for greasing
soft herbs, chopped, 1 tablespoon,
(my favourite mix is basil, chives and dill)
parmesan, finely grated, 1 tablespoon
+ a little extra for sprinkling
free-range egg 1
salt and freshly ground black pepper
cream 1 tablespoon

These baked eggs are such a treat for breakfast, served with buttered toast fingers to dip into the yolks encased in a creamy herb sauce. This is my favourite weekend breakfast. If you can, I recommend adding a little fresh dill — it goes superbly with eggs. Because ovens vary, I recommend checking on the eggs to see if they are cooked to your liking.

1 Preheat oven to 180°C. Butter medium-sized ramekin/s.

2 Sprinkle chopped herbs and parmesan in the ramekin/s.

3 Use a teaspoon to make a little dent in the middle of the herbs and parmesan, then crack in egg. Season with salt and pepper, drizzle with cream and sprinkle with extra parmesan.

4 Transfer ramekin/s to a baking dish. Pour hot water from the tap into the baking dish until it comes half to two-thirds of the way up the sides of the ramekin/s.

5 Bake for 15–20 minutes depending on whether you want runny or firmer yolks (15 minutes for runny, 20 minutes for firmer yolks — I love mine runny with the whites *juuuuust* set). Check after 15 minutes and give the dishes a little jiggle to see how cooked the eggs are; keep cooking for another 1–2 minutes or until they're done just to your liking.

6 Garnish with more fresh herbs and enjoy with buttered toast.

ENERGY	CARBS	PROTEIN
612kj / 146kcal	0.9g	9.7g

FAT	SAT FAT	SUGARS
11.8g	5.9g	0.7g

Spiced turmeric latte

fresh turmeric 3cm piece, peeled
(or ¾ teaspoon ground turmeric)
fresh ginger 2cm piece, peeled
honey 1 heaped teaspoon
**almond, cashew nut or hazelnut
    butter** 2 tablespoons
water 1½ cups (or milk for a
creamier drink)
ground cinnamon ½ teaspoon
black pepper pinch of
vanilla essence or extract 1 teaspoon
salt pinch of

Turmeric, cinnamon, ginger and creamy nut butter make this a warming, nourishing hot drink. I would drink this over a coffee any day! Turmeric is such a rock star ingredient with its antioxidant, anti-inflammatory and anti-bacterial properties. Use milk instead of water for an even creamier drink. The nut butter helps create a creamy froth on top of the latte (just like the creamy frothy part on top of a coffee latte or cappuccino).

1 Place all ingredients in a blender and blend until smooth and frothy. If you don't have a powerful blender, you may need to strain it to remove any bits that haven't blended completely.

2 Warm up in a small pot and pour into mugs. Sprinkle with more cinnamon to serve.

ENERGY	CARBS	PROTEIN	FAT	SAT FAT	SUGARS
412kj / 99kcal	5.9g	2.7g	7g	0.5g	3.7g

Choco-nut smoothie

SERVES 2 **PREP TIME** 5 minutes

GF | DF (use DF milk)

bananas (frozen) 2
avocado (just ripe) ½ small
peanut butter 3–4 tablespoons
dark cocoa or cacao powder
2–3 tablespoons
milk (of any kind) 2 cups
maple syrup 1 tablespoon (optional,
if you like it sweeter)
ice cubes 4–5
cacao nibs or grated chocolate,
to garnish (optional)

*Peanutty, chocolatey, thick, creamy AND good for you,
this smoothie is perfect for breakfast on the run, a post-
exercise snack, or when it comes to 3pm and you feel like
sneaking a chocolate bar! Kids LOVE this — it's a perfect
after-school treat that will keep them happy until dinner
time, and satisfy any sweet cravings while providing
healthy fats and protein.*

1 Blend everything together until smooth and pour into
glasses. Sprinkle with cacao nibs or chocolate if desired,
and guzzle away!

ENERGY	CARBS	PROTEIN	FAT	SAT FAT	SUGARS
2162kj / 517kcal	46.2g	19.2g	27.1g	6.6g	42.1g

Brunch salad

SERVES 2 **PREP TIME** 15 minutes
COOK TIME 10 minutes

GF (use GF bread) **| DF** (use mayo instead of yoghurt)

BACON, MUSHROOM AND TOMATO BRUNCH SALAD

portobello mushrooms 2 large or
4 smaller
tomatoes 2 large or 4 smaller, halved
streaky bacon 4–5 rashers
extra-virgin olive oil 1 tablespoon
balsamic vinegar 1 tablespoon
thyme leaves, chopped, 2 teaspoons

OR

SMOKED SALMON AND ASPARAGUS BRUNCH SALAD

asparagus 1 bunch (about 8 spears)
cold-smoked salmon 4 slices

DRESSING

garlic 1 small clove, minced
parsley, finely chopped, 2–3 tablespoons
mayonnaise 1 tablespoon
natural unsweetened yoghurt
2 tablespoons
extra-virgin olive oil 1 tablespoon
lemon juice of ½

TO SERVE

free-range eggs 2–4 (depending on if
you want 1 or 2 eggs each)
wholegrain toast bread 2 pieces
cos lettuce leaves of 1
avocado (just ripe) ½, sliced

It's got everything you want for a scrumptious weekend brunch, in salad form! Choose from either a bacon, mushroom and tomato salad, or a smoked salmon and asparagus salad.

1 Preheat oven grill to high. Bring a full kettle to the boil.

2 Place mushrooms (gill-side up), tomatoes (cut-side up) and bacon in a large baking dish or oven tray. Mix olive oil, balsamic vinegar and thyme together and spoon over mushrooms and tomatoes. Season with salt and pepper.

3 Grill for about 10 minutes or until bacon is crispy and mushrooms are soft. Alternatively, toss asparagus with a drizzle of olive oil, season with salt and pepper, and grill for 8–10 minutes until tender.

4 Meanwhile, whisk all dressing ingredients together and set aside. Pour boiling water into a fry pan on medium heat. Carefully crack eggs into simmering water and poach for about 2 minutes or until whites are just set but yolks are still runny. Put the bread in the toaster.

5 Arrange lettuce on serving plates and dress with half of the dressing. Top with avocado, grilled mushrooms, tomatoes and bacon OR grilled asparagus and smoked salmon. Remove poached eggs with a slotted spoon and place on top of salad. Butter toast, then chop and scatter over the salad. Dress with remaining dressing and season with salt and freshly ground black pepper. Brunch is served!

	ENERGY	CARBS	PROTEIN	FAT	SAT FAT	SUGARS
Bacon mushroom and tomato	2374kj / 568kcal	18.8g	26.2g	13.1g	6.6g	7.9g
Smoked salmon and asparagus	2798kj / 669kcal	14.3g	43.3g	36.8g	7.3g	3.6g

Let's eat!

LUNCH +

ROASTS. CURRIES. BAKES. BARBECUE. FAMILY FAVS. SLOW COOKS.
PIZZA. PASTA . . . THE LIST GOES ON

DINNER

Chicken banh mi with turmeric aïoli

MAKES 4 **PREP TIME** 20 minutes

DF (without pâté)

PICKLED VEGETABLES
vinegar (e.g. rice vinegar, apple cider vinegar or white wine vinegar) ½ cup
sugar 2 teaspoons
carrot 1 large, peeled and cut into thin matchsticks
red onion 1 small or ½ medium, peeled and thinly sliced
baby radishes 3–4, thinly sliced

TURMERIC AÏOLI
mayonnaise ¼ cup
ground turmeric 1 teaspoon
kaffir lime leaf 1, central stem removed, finely chopped (or 1 stalk lemongrass, very finely chopped) (optional)
lime or lemon juice 1 tablespoon
garlic 1 clove, minced
sweet chilli sauce 2 teaspoons

TO SERVE
French bread/baguette 1 loaf, cut into 4 pieces
chicken liver pâté ¼ cup (optional)
cooked chicken 400g, shredded
Lebanese cucumber 1, sliced
mint leaves ½–1 cup
coriander ½–1 cup
pickled jalapeños or other chillies

This ultimate street food sandwich is a result of the historic French influence in Vietnam — crusty French bread spread with pâté and a delicious creamy aïoli, filled with chicken or pork, pickled vegetables, chilli and loads of fresh herbs (a key part you can't skimp on!). This is a great one to feed a crowd or bring on a picnic — roast a whole chicken (or buy a pre-roasted one) and lay out all the fillings for everyone to make their own banh mi.

1 Mix vinegar and sugar together in a large bowl or dish; add carrot, onion and radish and toss in the vinegar mixture. Leave to pickle for at least 30 minutes (or overnight in the fridge).

2 Mix all Turmeric Aïoli ingredients together.

3 Slice an opening in each piece of bread and spread with pâté, if using. Spread with aïoli and fill with chicken, pickled vegetables, cucumber, plenty of fresh herbs, and a few pickled jalapeños.

ENERGY	CARBS	PROTEIN	FAT	SAT FAT	SUGARS
1953kj / 467kcal	41g	31.9g	18.8g	4.8g	9.2g

Chilaquiles con pollo (fancy chicken nachos)

*The best way to describe chilaquiles
(pronounced 'chila-killeys') is as
fancy nachos. Instead of melted
cheese, they are topped with pico de
gallo (fresh salsa) and queso fresco
(a soft, creamy white cheese) which I
replace with feta. A great starter,
casual lunch or snack with mates
and beers; they're extremely tasty
and moreish!*

chicken thighs (boneless, skinless)
300–400g
mayonnaise 1½ tablespoons
chipotle sauce 1–2 tablespoons
(see Note)
plain corn chips 1 bag
avocado (firm ripe) 1 large
lemon juice of ½
salt a pinch
Pico de Gallo (see page 73) 1½–2 cups
sour cream 150g pottle
Tabasco sauce to taste
feta 50g
coriander, chopped, ¼–½ cup

1 Preheat oven to 200°C. Pat chicken dry with paper towels
and place in a baking dish.

2 Drizzle with olive oil and season with salt and pepper. Roast
for about 15 minutes or until just cooked through.

3 Leave chicken to cool, then shred meat with two forks. Toss
shredded meat with mayonnaise and chipotle sauce.

4 Arrange corn chips on a large plate. In a bowl, roughly mash
avocado with lemon juice and season to taste with salt.

5 Dollop shredded chicken mixture, avocado and Pico de Gallo
over corn chips. Dollop with sour cream and sprinkle on
Tabasco sauce. Crumble feta on top and scatter with coriander.
Serve with extra Pico de Gallo on the side.

Chipotle sauce is a
smoked Mexican chilli
sauce. It's become super
popular and widely
available in supermarkets
in either the International
or sauce section.

ENERGY	CARBS	PROTEIN	FAT	SAT FAT	SUGARS
2062kj / 493kcal	34g	17.2g	32.2g	12.8g	2.4g

Turmeric and ginger chicken soul soup

SERVES 4–6 **PREP TIME** 20 minutes **COOK TIME** 1 hour 20 minutes   **DF | GF**

chicken 1 whole (size 14 or 16)
water 1.75 litres
salt 1 teaspoon
olive oil 2 tablespoons
white part of leek 1, diced (or 1 onion, diced)
carrots 2, peeled and diced
butternut (or pumpkin), peeled and diced, 2 cups
garlic 2 cloves, chopped
ground turmeric 1 teaspoon
fresh ginger 2.5cm piece, peeled and grated
greens (e.g. baby spinach, spinach or silverbeet leaves) 120–150g, roughly chopped
lemon juice of ½
parsley, finely chopped, ¼ cup
salt and pepper

This simple, nourishing chicken soup is total soul food — it's perfect to make and eat when you are in need of a little TLC. I simmer a whole chicken to make stock (SO much more flavoursome than any bought stock or concentrate), then add the chicken meat and the rest of the ingredients to create the most simple but delicious bowl of goodness.

1 Place whole chicken in a large pot, cover with water and add salt. Cover and bring to the boil. Reduce heat and simmer, partially covered, for about 1 hour or until chicken is just cooked. Remove chicken and set aside to cool. Strain the stock into another large pot or bowl and set aside.

2 Heat olive oil in a large pot (you could use the one the chicken was cooked in) and cook leek, carrot and butternut until soft. Add garlic, turmeric and ginger and continue cooking for 2–3 minutes.

3 Add 1.5 litres of the strained chicken stock and simmer for 8–10 minutes or until vegetables are tender. Meanwhile, shred chicken meat off the carcass.

4 Stir greens and shredded chicken into the soup with lemon juice and parsley. Season to taste with salt and pepper.

ENERGY	CARBS	PROTEIN	FAT	SAT FAT	SUGARS
1311kj / 314kcal	6.2g	30.7g	18.1g	5g	4.9g

Chipotle charred chicken

SERVES 4–6 **PREP TIME** 15 minutes (+ 30 minutes marinating time)
COOK TIME 35–45 minutes

DF (without jalapeño cream) | **GF**

chicken 1 whole (size 14 or 16)
chipotle sauce ¼ cup + 2 tablespoons
(see Note)
red onions 2 large, cut into 3cm-thick
wedges
olive oil
salt
coriander, roughly chopped,
¼ cup, to garnish
lime 1, cut into wedges, to serve

JALAPEÑO CREAM
**sour cream or unsweetened natural
  yoghurt** ½ cup
mint, parsley and/or coriander,
chopped, ¼ cup
lime juice of 1 (or ½ lemon)
pickled jalapeños ¼ cup, chopped

Note

Find chipotle sauce
(a smoked Mexican
chilli sauce) in the
sauces or international
foods section of the
supermarket.

*Super-fast to prepare and super tasty, this is a winner of
a chicken dinner for anyone who loves smoky Mexican
flavours. It will surprise you how easy it can be to make a
dinner so delicious with such little effort when you've got
a bottle of chipotle sauce in the fridge (a very handy
thing to have!). Either buy a chicken that's already been
butterflied (for extra ease) or butterfly it yourself using
the method below.*

1 Preheat a hooded barbecue to medium heat.
Alternatively, preheat oven to 220°C. Pat chicken dry with
paper towels. To butterfly the chicken, place breast-side
down on a chopping board. Use sharp kitchen scissors to
cut down either side of the back-bone, from the cavity
opening end right down to the neck. Discard the back-
bone (or reserve it to make stock). Turn chicken over (so
it's now breast-side up) and push it down flat with both
hands — you may hear the breastbones crack a little.

2 Spread chicken generously with ¼ cup chipotle sauce
and leave to marinate at room temperature for about
30 minutes (or a few hours in the fridge, then bring to
room temperature when ready to cook).

3 Place marinated chicken on two large pieces of tinfoil
lined with baking paper (or in a roasting dish, if using the
oven). Fold the edges of the tinfoil up to make a 'tray'
(which will help to catch all the yummy juices). Arrange
onion wedges around chicken, and drizzle with remaining
2 tablespoons chipotle sauce. Drizzle chicken and onions
with olive oil and season with salt. Cook chicken for 35–40
minutes, hood down (if using barbecue) or until just
cooked through and the juices run clear. Remove and set
aside, covered, to rest for 10–15 minutes.

4 Mix all Jalapeño Cream ingredients together. Serve
carved chicken, garnished with coriander, with lime
wedges to squeeze over, onions and Jalapeño Cream.

ENERGY	CARBS	PROTEIN	FAT	SAT FAT	SUGARS
1262kj / 302kcal	5.8g	30.5g	17.5g	7.2g	5.2g

Italian chicken, tomato, pumpkin and mozzarella bake

SERVES 6 **PREP TIME** 30 minutes **COOK TIME** 35 minutes   *GF*

chicken thighs (boneless, skinless)
800g, at room temperature
dried mixed herbs or oregano
1½ teaspoons
lemon zest of 1
olive oil 2 tablespoons
pumpkin (or butternut) 600–700g,
cut into 1–2cm cubes (you can leave the
skin on)
red onion 1, chopped
garlic 4 cloves, chopped
thyme leaves (or rosemary leaves),
2 teaspoons, finely chopped
olive oil
salt and pepper
crushed tomatoes (or cherry tomatoes)
2 x 400g cans
tomato paste 2 tablespoons
sugar 2 teaspoons
red wine vinegar 2 tablespoons
roasted red capsicum 1 large (from a jar
or the deli), sliced
capers (or chopped olives)
2 tablespoons, drained
white wine or chicken stock ⅓ cup
mozzarella, grated, 1 cup
basil leaves or flat-leaf parsley
a small handful, to garnish

ENERGY		CARBS	
1471kj / 352kcal		15.9g	

PROTEIN	FAT	SAT FAT	SUGARS
34.5g	14.9g	5.4g	12.3g

You can't beat a comforting humble chicken bake!

1 Preheat oven to 200°C. Line an oven tray with baking paper. Pat chicken dry with paper towels. Mix dried herbs, lemon zest and olive oil in a large bowl or dish, add chicken and toss to coat. Leave to marinate at room temperature for 15–20 minutes.

2 In prepared tray, toss pumpkin, onion and garlic with thyme, a good drizzle of olive oil, and season with salt and pepper. Roast for about 20 minutes or until slightly caramelised.

3 Stir tomatoes, tomato paste, sugar and vinegar together in a pot and simmer for about 10 minutes until slightly reduced. Season to taste with salt, pepper and a good glug of olive oil. Stir in roasted capsicum and capers.

4 Season marinated chicken with salt. Heat a drizzle of olive oil in a large fry pan on medium heat. Brown chicken in batches, on both sides (but you don't have to cook it right through) and set aside. Add wine or stock to the pan and allow to bubble for a minute or two while you use a wooden spoon to rub the bottom of the pan to release all the pan brownings (there's tonnes of flavour in this so you don't want it to go to waste!)

5 Arrange chicken and vegetables in a roasting dish or large baking dish. Pour wine reduction from the pan over the chicken. Spoon sauce on top and scatter with mozzarella. Bake for 8–10 minutes, then switch to grill for 2–3 minutes or until cheese is bubbly and golden.

6 Scatter basil or parsley on top. Serve with steamed green veg such as beans or broccoli (for a winter meal) or a leafy green salad (for a summer meal) and mashed potato, creamy polenta or pasta.

Pistachio-crumbed chicken schnitzel with Turkish salad

SERVES 4 **PREP TIME** 20 minutes **COOK TIME** 20 minutes

DF (omit feta) | **GF**

PISTACHIO-CRUMBED CHICKEN SCHNITZEL

pistachios, shelled, ⅔ cup
sesame seeds 2½ tablespoons
sumac 1 tablespoon (optional) (see Note)
salt 1 teaspoon
chicken breast (boneless, skinless) 4
oil 2–3 tablespoons

TURKISH SALAD

telegraph cucumber 1, diced
cherry tomatoes 1 punnet (about 250g), cut in half
red onion ½, thinly sliced
avocado (firm ripe) 1, sliced
mint leaves ½ cup, torn
feta 100g, crumbled
lemons juice of 1½
salt and pepper

TO SERVE

hummus 1 cup, warmed

Note

You can find sumac (a lemony-tasting dried and ground berry) in the spice section of many supermarkets these days. However, if you can't find it, use finely grated lemon zest instead.

Pistachios and sesame seeds make a delicious golden crunchy, nutty (and gluten-free) coating for these chicken schnitzels. If you can't find sumac (a dried, ground berry), just use lemon zest in its place for the same lemony flavour.

1 Preheat oven to 180°C. Briefly blitz pistachios in a food processor until finely chopped. Alternatively, just finely chop them by hand on a chopping board. Mix with sesame seeds, sumac (if using) and salt in a dish.

2 Pat chicken dry with paper towels and slice chicken breasts in half horizontally to make thin schnitzel pieces (to do this, lay a chicken breast on a chopping board and place one hand flat on top to hold it steady while you cut through with the knife in your other hand very carefully).

3 Coat each schnitzel liberally with pistachio mixture.

4 Heat oil in a large fry pan (preferably non-stick) on medium heat. Cook schnitzels in batches, for about 2 minutes on each side, until golden brown, then transfer to an oven dish and finish off cooking in oven for 5 minutes.

5 Combine all salad ingredients and season with a little salt and pepper. Warm hummus.

6 To serve, arrange chicken schnitzels and salad on plates and serve with a good dollop of hummus on the side.

ENERGY	CARBS	PROTEIN	FAT	SAT FAT	SUGARS
3039kj / 727kcal	16g	55.9g	47.4g	10.2g	7.7g

Pumpkin and carrot butter chicken

SERVES 4 **PREP TIME** 25 minutes **COOK TIME** 20 minutes

DF (use coconut cream + yoghurt) | **GF**

chicken thighs (boneless, skinless)
600–700g
onion 1, finely chopped
**garam masala, ground cumin, smoked
  paprika** 1 tablespoon of each
ground coriander, ground turmeric
1 teaspoon of each
ground chilli ¼–½ teaspoon (optional)
garlic 2 cloves, minced
fresh ginger, finely grated, 2 teaspoons
lemon zest of ½
salt 1 teaspoon
cooking oil a good drizzle
butternut pumpkin, grated, 1½–2 cups
carrot 1, grated
crushed tomatoes 400g can
tomato paste 2–3 tablespoons
cream (or coconut cream) ½–⅔ cup
salt and pepper
natural unsweetened yoghurt (dairy or
coconut) 3 tablespoons

TO SERVE
natural unsweetened yoghurt (dairy or
coconut) ¼ cup
coriander, chopped, ¼ cup

*Here's my (much healthier and delicious) take on the
takeaway favourite. It's got the same lovely creamy, mildly
spiced, tomato flavour, but is packed with veges and has
much less fat and sugar. Adding grated vegetables to curry
is a great way to get everyone eating more vegetables, and
the pumpkin and carrot add a subtle natural sweetness to
this mild curry.*

1 Pat chicken dry with paper towels then cut into 2–3cm
cubes. Combine with onion, spices, garlic, ginger, lemon zest
and salt.

2 Heat a good drizzle of oil in a large fry pan on medium
heat. Add chicken, onion and spices, and cook for about
10–12 minutes or until starting to brown (the chicken doesn't
have to be cooked through yet). If at any time the chicken
and spices are catching on the bottom of the pan and
burning, add a few tablespoons of water and stir.

3 Stir in grated pumpkin, carrot, tomatoes, tomato paste and
cream. Simmer for 5–10 minutes or until sauce is reduced
slightly and chicken is cooked through. Season to taste with
salt and pepper.

4 Remove from heat and stir through yoghurt.

5 Garnish with more yoghurt and coriander. Serve with rice
and Cucumber Mint Salad (page 138) or Coconut Green
Beans (page 142) as a shared meal.

ENERGY	CARBS	PROTEIN	FAT	SAT FAT	SUGARS
1464kj / 350kcal	14.1g	35.9g	15.9g	8.9g	11.5g

My Malaysian chicken rendang

SERVES 4–6 **PREP TIME** 20 minutes **COOK TIME** 40–45 minutes

DF | GF (use GF soy sauce)

SPICE PASTE
red chillies 2 large
shallots 3 large, peeled and chopped
onion 1, peeled and chopped
garlic 2 cloves, peeled and chopped
dried chillies 2, soaked in hot water for
a few minutes (or 1 teaspoon chilli flakes)
ground turmeric 1½ teaspoons
ground coriander 1 tablespoon
ground cumin 1 tablespoon
fresh ginger 3cm piece, peeled and
chopped
lemongrass stalks, finely sliced, ¼ cup
kaffir lime leaves 2, central stem
removed, shredded
salt ¾ teaspoon
oil 2 tablespoons

CURRY
coconut milk 400ml can
free-range chicken 1 whole, size 14 or
16, jointed (or 1.5–1.7kg chicken pieces,
preferably with the bones in, e.g.
drumsticks, thighs)
water ½ cup
soy sauce 1 tablespoon
tamarind juice ½ cup (see Note)
desiccated coconut 1 cup
salt

Note

To make tamarind juice, mix tamarind paste
or pulp with boiling water according to
packet instructions. Tamarind is sold in the
international section of many supermarkets,
but, if you can't get hold of it, just use ¼ cup
water mixed with ¼ cup lemon juice and
1 teaspoon brown sugar. It has the same tart
and sweet flavour.

Rendang is a rich, fragrant and spicy Malaysian curry of chicken (or beef) cooked in spices and coconut milk, with the added flavour and texture of desiccated coconut. It's a dry curry (so it's not very saucy) — a result of reducing the coconut milk to intensify the richness and flavour. At any celebratory gathering we went to when I was growing up in Malaysia, it would always be part of the feast.

1 Blend all spice paste ingredients in a high-speed blender or food processor until smooth.

2 Heat a drizzle of oil in a wok or large pot on medium heat. Cook spice paste for 2–3 minutes until fragrant, stirring frequently, then stir in ¼ cup of the coconut milk and continue cooking for a further 2 minutes.

3 Add chicken and stir to coat in spice paste. Stir in remaining coconut milk, water, soy sauce and tamarind juice. Cook, covered, for 5–10 minutes, then remove lid and simmer for about 30 minutes or until the sauce has reduced by more than half and chicken is tender. Stir a few times during cooking to make sure the sauce is not sticking to the bottom of the pan and burning. If you think it is reducing too fast, just add a little more water.

4 Meanwhile toast desiccated coconut in a dry fry pan (no oil), on medium heat, for a few minutes, stirring frequently to avoid burning, until lightly coloured and fragrant. Stir toasted coconut into curry in the last 5 minutes of cooking. Check seasoning and add a little more salt if needed.

5 Garnish with more sliced chilli and shredded kaffir lime leaf, if you like. Serve with rice and steamed greens or Cucumber Mint Salad (page 138).

ENERGY	CARBS
2990kj / 715kcal	14.1g

PROTEIN	FAT	SAT FAT	SUGARS
49.7g	51.4g	29.1g	5.9g

Dad's nasi lemak

SERVES 6 **PREP TIME** 25 minutes **COOK TIME** 30 minutes

DF | GF

COCONUT RICE
jasmine rice 2 cups
coconut milk 2 cups
water 1¼ cups
salt a good pinch

QUICK PRAWN SAMBAL
chilli sauce (or sambal oelek)
3 tablespoons
brown sugar 2½ teaspoons
tamarind juice (see Note on page 50)
½ cup
oil 3 tablespoons
shallots 2–3 large (or 6 small), peeled
and finely sliced
shelled prawns (with tails left on)
350–400g
kaffir lime leaf ½, central stem removed,
finely shredded (optional)
lime juice of 1

BITS AND PIECES TO SERVE
telegraph cucumber 1, sliced
free-range eggs 4–6, hard-boiled,
shells removed and halved
roasted peanuts ¾ cup
dried anchovies (ikan billis), deep-fried
(optional)
My Malaysian Chicken Rendang
(page 50) (optional)

My dad is Malaysian and whenever we would visit his home country, one of the first things we'd eat is nasi lemak. It's considered the national dish — you find it everywhere you go in Malaysia and people eat it for breakfast, lunch and dinner! Basically, it's rice cooked in coconut milk (yum!) with lots of tasty condiments such as prawn sambal, deep-fried ikan billis (little anchovies) and peanuts, cucumber and hard-boiled egg. Sometimes it is also served with a chicken or beef rendang curry for an extra-special meal.

1 Combine all Coconut Rice ingredients in a pot, cover with a lid and bring to the boil. As soon as it boils, reduce to very low heat and cook for 15 minutes. Turn off heat and leave to steam, still covered, for a further 10 minutes.

2 To make the Quick Prawn Sambal, mix chilli sauce, brown sugar and tamarind juice together. Place oil and shallots in a large fry pan on medium heat. Bring to a sizzle and cook shallots for 4–5 minutes or until soft and just starting to colour. If, at any time, it looks like they're starting to burn, add a splash of water to the pan and stir.

3 Pat prawns dry with paper towels; add to shallots in pan and cook for 2 minutes. Stir in chilli sauce mixture, kaffir lime leaf (if using) and lime juice. Simmer for 3–5 minutes until sauce is thick. Season to taste with salt and more lime juice and sugar if needed.

4 Serve Quick Prawn Sambal with Coconut Rice and all the condiments, and chicken rendang for an extra-special meal.

ENERGY	CARBS	PROTEIN	FAT	SAT FAT	SUGARS
2924kj / 699kcal	67.1g	35.9g	35g	15.6g	8.7g

Caribbean marinade (for chicken or pork)

MAKES ¾–1 cup **PREP TIME** 15 minutes   **DF | GF** (use GF soy sauce)

If you like a fiery barbecue marinade, then you need this recipe in your life! The amount (and type) of chilli you use is up to you depending on how fiery you want it to be (if not at all, you can still make it with a mild chilli or two and the seeds taken out). It makes incredibly tasty barbecued chicken thighs, amazing served with mango salsa. But you can use it to marinade anything from fish to vegetables to pork or steak.

CARIBBEAN MARINADE

spring onions 3–4, chopped
thyme leaves 3 tablespoons, chopped
fresh ginger 2.5cm piece, peeled and chopped
garlic 4 cloves, chopped
ground allspice 1 tablespoon
brown sugar 2 tablespoons
limes juice of 2 (or juice of 1 lemon)
tomato paste 1 tablespoon
soy sauce 1 tablespoon
oil 3–4 tablespoons
red chillies 2 large, chopped
salt 1 teaspoon

Storage

The marinade will keep for up to 2 weeks in the fridge or can be frozen for months.

1 Blend all ingredients together in a food processor or blender until well combined. Use to marinate meat and chicken, as in the recipes below.

Caribbean chicken 'n salsa

SERVES 4–6

Marinate 600–800g boneless, skinless **chicken thighs** or breast in ¾–1 cup **Caribbean Marinade** for an hour or overnight. Season with **salt** and grill or barbecue until cooked through. Serve with Coconut Rice (see page 52) and a salsa made from 1 fresh **mango**, diced, 3–4 **tomatoes**, diced, 1 **red capsicum**, cored and thinly sliced, 1 **Lebanese cucumber**, diced, 2 **spring onions**, finely sliced, ¼ cup **toasted shredded coconut**, ½ cup chopped **basil or coriander**, juice of 1 **lime** or ½ **lemon**, and a drizzle of **extra-virgin olive oil**.

Caribbean pork chops 'n salsa

SERVES 4–6

Marinate 8–10 **pork chops** in ¾–1 cup **Caribbean Marinade** for an hour or overnight. Season with **salt** and cook on barbecue or pan-fry for 2–3 minutes each side, then cover with barbecue hood or finish off cooking in a 200°C oven for 4–5 minutes or until just cooked through. Serve with **mango salsa** (above).

	ENERGY	CARBS	PROTEIN	FAT	SAT FAT	SUGARS
chicken	1940kj / 464kcal	22.3g	36.8g	24.6g	6.9g	21g
pork	2171kj / 519kcal	22.3g	53.4g	23.3g	6.9g	21g

Thai whole baked fish

SERVES 4 **PREP TIME** 5 minutes **COOK TIME** 20–30 minutes   **DF | GF** (use GF soy sauce)

whole fish about 1.8kg (either 1 large or
2 medium, e.g. snapper, terakihi,
John Dory or flounder; gutted, scaled
and cleaned)
Sticky Chilli Sauce, page 156 (or sweet
chilli sauce) ⅓ cup
lemongrass, finely chopped or grated,
1 tablespoon
kaffir lime leaves 2, finely chopped
(or zest of 2 limes)
fish sauce (or soy sauce)
1½ tablespoons
ground turmeric ½ teaspoon
coconut cream ¼ cup
salt to season

TO SERVE
coriander, roughly chopped, ½ cup
lime 1, cut into wedges

*There's something about delivering a whole cooked fish to
the table — it makes a real statement about cooking simply,
naturally and respecting your ingredients. Plus, it makes a
beautiful centrepiece! Use my Sticky Chilli Sauce (page 156)
— or, if you're short on time, some shop-bought sweet chilli
sauce will do — mixed with the other ingredients to make a
glaze. It caramelises in the oven and goes sticky and delicious.
If the thought of cooking a whole fish is slightly scary, just use
boneless fillets of fish (and reduce cook time to 8–10 minutes),
it will be just as delicious.*

1 Preheat oven to 220°C. Pat fish dry with paper towels. Use a
sharp knife to slash fish in a criss-cross pattern on both sides.

2 Mix Sticky Chilli Sauce with lemongrass, kaffir lime leaves,
fish sauce, turmeric and coconut cream. Slather all over the
fish on both sides, getting into the cuts and a little into the
cavity. Season with salt.

3 Bake for 20–30 minutes or until fish is just cooked through
and flesh flakes away easily. Garnish with coriander. Serve
with lime wedges (to squeeze over), Coconut Rice (page 52)
and green vegetables or salad.

ENERGY	CARBS		
1103kj / 264kcal	18.4g		

PROTEIN	FAT	SAT FAT	SUGARS
31.6g	7.8g	3.7g	15.6g

Pan-fried fish with asparagus, brown butter and lemon

SERVES 2 **PREP TIME** 10 minutes **COOK TIME** 10 minutes

GF

olive oil for cooking
asparagus 1 bunch (about 8–10 spears), trimmed
fresh white fish fillets (preferably skin on) 300–350g
salt and pepper
butter 25g
capers 1 teaspoon, patted dry with paper towels
juicy lemon juice of 1
dill, chopped, 2 teaspoons

Tips

• For crispy skin, make sure your fish is dry (patted dry with paper towels) and use a fish slice to press down gently on fish while cooking in the pan, skin-side down (to help the whole fillet make surface contact with the pan) until it relaxes and the fish is flat.
• Once you've cooked the skin-side and flipped it over, you really only need to let the flesh 'kiss' the hot pan for about 1 minute (or slightly longer if they're thick fillets). When you take the fish out of the pan, it will continue cooking for a little longer.

My favourite, and one of the simplest, ways to cook fresh fish fillets. You can't go wrong with butter and lemon when you've got fresh fish, but add some capers and fresh herbs and it becomes even more superb! When the butter starts to bubble and turn brown, it gives a delicious nutty, sweet flavour that makes the fish and asparagus sing!

1 Heat a good drizzle of olive oil in a large fry pan on medium-high heat. Cook asparagus for 4–5 minutes or until just tender. Add a couple of tablespoons of water to the pan to help it steam and cook through. Set asparagus aside, keep pan on the heat.

2 Pat fish dry with paper towels and season with salt and pepper. Add another drizzle of oil to the pan. Cook fish, skin-side-down first, for about 2 minutes. Flip fish over to cook the other side, then add butter and capers to pan — the butter will melt and start to turn brown. Just as it starts doing this, squeeze in the lemon juice. As it starts to bubble, spoon the lemon and caper butter over the fish.

3 Return asparagus to the pan, turn off the heat and sprinkle everything with dill.

4 Serve with boiled baby spuds or good old mash.

ENERGY	CARBS	PROTEIN	FAT	SAT FAT	SUGARS
1087kj / 260kcal	2.9g	35.3g	11.8g	7.2g	2.6g

Pomegranate-glazed salmon, pink pickled onions, caper and dill crème

SERVES 6–8 **PREP TIME** 10 minutes **COOK TIME** 20–25 minutes   **DF** (without crème fraîche) **| GF**

A whole side of salmon is an extra-special dish that is perfect to serve for a dinner party, special lunch or at Christmas time. It's easy and quick to make and looks very impressive. The sharp fruity flavour of pomegranate helps to cut through the richness of the salmon, and the pink pickled onions and dill crème take it up another notch in the special dining ranks. If you don't have pomegranate molasses, make your own glaze using balsamic vinegar and pomegranate or cranberry juice (see Tip).

red wine vinegar ¼ cup
sugar 1 teaspoon
red onion 1, halved and thinly sliced
fresh salmon (skin on or off) 1 side, pin-boned
pomegranate molasses 3 tablespoons (or see Tip)
salt and freshly ground black pepper

CAPER AND DILL CRÈME
crème fraîche 200g
lemon zest and juice of ½
capers, chopped, 2 tablespoons
dill, chopped, 2 teaspoons

1 Preheat oven to 180°C. In a medium-sized bowl, mix vinegar with sugar. Add sliced onion and toss. Leave to marinate for 20 minutes (or overnight) in the fridge.

2 Pat salmon dry with paper towels. Lay, flesh-side up, on a large oven tray lined with baking paper. Rub or brush pomegranate molasses all over salmon and season generously with salt and freshly ground black pepper. Bake for 20 minutes, then grill for a final 2 minutes (to get a little caramelisation).

3 To make the Caper and Dill Crème, mix crème fraîche, lemon zest and juice, capers and dill together, season with a little salt and freshly ground black pepper.

4 Transfer salmon to a large serving platter. Drain pickled red onions and scatter over the salmon. Serve Caper and Dill Crème in a small bowl on the side.

Tip

To make your own glaze, simply boil ¾ cup pomegranate or cranberry juice, 2 tablespoons balsamic vinegar and 1½ tablespoons brown sugar together in a small saucepan for about 8–10 minutes or until reduced to a syrup. It will thicken as it cools.

ENERGY	CARBS	PROTEIN	FAT	SAT FAT	SUGARS
1633kj / 391kcal	3.5g	30.6g	27.5g	11.9g	3g

60

Super sushi

MAKES about 30 pieces of sushi **SERVES** 4
PREP TIME 30 minutes **COOK TIME** 25 minutes

DF | GF (use GF soy sauce)

SUPER-GRAIN RICE

short-grain sushi rice ¾ cup
quinoa ¾ cup (I like to use a mix of red
and black quinoa, but any quinoa is fine)
water 2¼ cups
salt a good pinch
Japanese rice vinegar 1½ tablespoons
mirin 2 teaspoons (or, if you don't have
mirin, use 1 teaspoon sugar)

TO ASSEMBLE AND SERVE

fresh salmon fillet 500g, skin removed,
pin-boned
telegraph cucumber ½ large
avocado (just ripe) flesh of 1 large
nori seaweed sheets 4
soy sauce
wasabi
pickled ginger

*I've called this super sushi because it's super good for you
with protein- and fibre-rich quinoa (which is mixed in with
the rice), omega 3-packed salmon, loads of healthy fats
from avocado and vitamins and minerals from crunchy
cucumber. It makes a super addition to the lunchbox to
take to work or school.*

1 Combine rice, quinoa, water and salt in a pot, cover and
bring to the boil. Reduce to lowest heat and simmer, covered,
for 15 minutes. Turn off heat and leave to steam, still covered,
for a further 8 minutes.

2 Spread cooked rice out on a tray or in a large dish and
sprinkle with vinegar and mirin (or sugar). Leave to cool, then
mix to distribute the vinegar and mirin through evenly.

3 Cut salmon into 1.5cm-wide strips. Cut cucumber in half,
then cut each half into quarters lengthways and cut out the
seeds. Cut each piece into three strips. Slice the avocado.

4 To roll the sushi, place a sheet of nori on a clean, dry, flat
surface (bench or chopping board), making sure the rough
side of the nori is facing up. Wet your hands (to avoid sticky
fingers) and make a good handful of rice into a ball. Place in
the middle and gently spread it (don't compress it) equally
over the nori, creating a layer of rice that covers almost all the
nori, except a 2cm margin at the top (you'll see why you need
this empty space when you come to rolling the sushi!).

5 Arrange strips of cucumber, salmon and avocado along the
length of the nori closest to you. Roll the nori and rice over
the filling, enclosing it firmly, then continue rolling with gentle
pressure so that the roll is nice and tight. When you get to
the 2cm margin at the top, dip your finger in water and
wet the strip of nori ever so slightly. Then continue rolling to
close the sushi — the damp nori will stick to the rest of the
roll. Repeat with remaining nori, quinoa rice and fillings.

6 Use a sharp, clean knife to cut each roll into 6–8 pieces.
Serve with soy sauce, wasabi and pickled ginger.

ENERGY	**CARBS**		
2457kj / 588kcal	45.3g		
PROTEIN	**FAT**	**SAT FAT**	**SUGARS**
34.9g	28.9g	6.7g	1.6g

Harissa (for fish or chickpea salad)

MAKES ¾–1 cup   **PREP TIME** 5–10 minutes   **DF** (without yoghurt) | **GF**

If you like big bold flavours, then you have to have a good harissa recipe up your sleeve. The blend of spices, garlic, lemon and chillies instantly adds a truckload of flavour to any chicken, meat, fish or vegetable dish. Use it as a marinade (especially if you're barbecuing), as a base for curries, casseroles or even as a condiment (it's fantastic mixed with yoghurt for a dipping or side sauce).

garlic 3 cloves, chopped
red chillies 1–2 large, chopped
cumin seeds 2½ teaspoons, crushed
coriander seeds 2 teaspoons, crushed
brown sugar 1 teaspoon
lemon juice of ½
salt 1 teaspoon
tomato paste 3–4 tablespoons
olive oil 3–4 tablespoons

Storage

Store in the fridge. Will keep for up to 2 weeks or can be frozen for months.

1 Blend all ingredients together in a food processor or blender until well combined. Alternatively, bash all ingredients, except tomato paste and olive oil, in a mortar and pestle until a paste, then mix in tomato paste and olive oil.

Harissa charred fish

SERVES 4–6

Smear ¾ cup **Harissa**, mixed with 1 tablespoon **olive oil**, all over 600–800g firm-fleshed **fish fillets**. Leave to marinate for 15–20 minutes. Heat a drizzle of oil on barbecue hotplate or in a large fry pan on medium heat. Season with **salt** and cook fish for about 2 minutes on one side, then carefully flip over and cook for 1–2 minutes on other side or until just cooked through. If using a fry pan, cook in batches to avoid overcrowding the pan. Drizzle any cooking juices from the pan over the fish, garnish with chopped **coriander or parsley**. Serve with **lemon wedges** and ¼ cup **unsweetened natural yoghurt** mixed with 1 tablespoon **Harissa**.

Chickpea salad with harissa yoghurt dressing

SERVES 4–6 as a side

Heat a drizzle of oil in a large fry pan. Add ¼ cup **Harissa** and cook for about 2 minutes, stirring with a wooden spoon. Add 2 x 400g cans **chickpeas** (rinsed, drained and patted dry with paper towels) and toss to coat. Turn off heat and toss with 2 **Lebanese cucumbers**, diced, 3–4 **tomatoes**, diced, ½ **red onion**, finely diced, and ½ cup roughly chopped **flat-leaf parsley**. Mix ¼ cup **unsweetened natural yoghurt** with 1 tablespoon **Harissa** paste and use to dress salad.

	ENERGY	CARBS	PROTEIN	FAT	SAT FAT	SUGARS
Harissa charred fish	1340kj / 321kcal	5.7g	32.2g	18.7g	3.4g	5.2g
Chickpea salad	889kj / 219kcal	21g	12.4g	8.7g	1.8g	7.3g

Slow-roasted lamb with secret salsa verde

SERVES 8–10 **PREP TIME** 15 minutes **COOK TIME** 3–4 hours + 20–30 minutes   **DF | GF**

lamb leg or shoulder 1 (about 2–2.5kg), brought up to room temperature
rosemary leaves, finely chopped, 3 tablespoons
garlic 3–4 cloves, minced
anchovies 2–3, finely chopped (optional, but recommended)
lemon zest of 1
olive oil 2 tablespoons
salt 1 teaspoon
freshly ground black pepper 1 teaspoon

SECRET SALSA VERDE
mint leaves 1 cup
thyme leaves 2 tablespoons
flat-leaf parsley, roughly chopped, ½ cup
anchovies 2–3 (optional, but recommended)
capers 2½ tablespoons
garlic 1 small clove, finely chopped
Dijon mustard 1–1½ teaspoons
lemon zest and juice of 1
extra-virgin olive oil ¼ cup

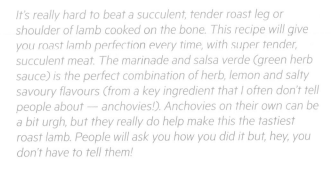

It's really hard to beat a succulent, tender roast leg or shoulder of lamb cooked on the bone. This recipe will give you roast lamb perfection every time, with super tender, succulent meat. The marinade and salsa verde (green herb sauce) is the perfect combination of herb, lemon and salty savoury flavours (from a key ingredient that I often don't tell people about — anchovies!). Anchovies on their own can be a bit urgh, but they really do help make this the tastiest roast lamb. People will ask you how you did it but, hey, you don't have to tell them!

1 Preheat oven to 220°C. Pat lamb dry with paper towels. Use a small, sharp knife to make lots of 1–2cm wide cuts all over the lamb (about 30–40 cuts in total). Mix rosemary, garlic, anchovies, lemon zest, olive oil, salt and pepper together. Rub this mixture all over the lamb, making sure you push some deeply into the cuts (to infuse the flavour).

2 Place lamb in a large roasting dish, on a rack, and roast for 15 minutes at 220°C, then reduce heat to 150°C and continue to cook for a further 3–4 hours or until the meat is very tender. Set aside to rest, covered with tinfoil and a few tea towels, for at least 20–30 minutes before serving.

3 To make the Secret Salsa Verde, place mint, thyme, parsley, anchovies, capers and garlic in a pile on a big, steady chopping board. Use a large knife to chop all the ingredients up finely together, mixing everything as you go. This method of making the sauce gives a much nicer texture and flavour than blending it. Transfer to a bowl and mix in mustard, lemon zest and juice, and olive oil. Season to taste with salt, freshly ground black pepper, and more lemon juice if required.

4 Slice lamb against the grain and serve with the Secret Salsa Verde on the side.

ENERGY	CARBS	PROTEIN	FAT	SAT FAT	SUGARS
2043kj / 489kcal	1.7g	59.9g	27.2g	8.9g	0.9g

Seriously good shanks with herb, lemon and walnut topping

SERVES 4–6 **PREP TIME** 20 minutes **COOK TIME** 10 minutes + 3 hours to slow cook

DF | GF (use GF flour)

hindquarter lamb shanks 4–6
plain flour 2 tablespoons
salt 1 teaspoon
olive oil for cooking
onion 1 large, diced
carrots 2, diced
garlic 4 cloves, chopped
smoked paprika 2 teaspoons
ground cumin 2 teaspoons
ground coriander 2 teaspoons
freshly ground black pepper
cinnamon stick 1 whole
tomato paste 2 tablespoons
crushed tomatoes 400g can
red wine ½ cup
chicken stock 1½–2 cups
dried apricots (or figs), roughly chopped, ½ cup

LEMON AND WALNUT TOPPING
walnuts, chopped, ¼ cup
coriander, chopped, ¼ cup
flat-leaf parsley, chopped, ¼ cup
lemon zest of 1
salt and pepper

Lemon and spinach couscous

Bring 1½ cups **chicken stock** to a boil in a small- to medium-sized pot. Take off the heat and stir in 1½ cups **couscous**, a generous knob (about 20g) of **butter** and zest of 1 **lemon**. Place a lid on top or cover with a plate, and leave to steam for 10 minutes. Uncover, fluff up with a fork and toss through 3 handfuls of chopped **spinach** until lightly wilted. Season to taste with **salt and pepper**.

These are seriously good shanks. I'm willing to bet you that these could be the best lamb shanks you've ever had. Everyone who has ever eaten them has said exactly that! With melt-in-your-mouth tender meat falling off the bone, a rich sauce with hints of warming spice and sweetness that you'll want to lick off the plate, and a vibrant touch of lemon and herbs at the end, this recipe will become your go-to over winter.

1 Preheat oven to 160°C. Pat shanks dry with paper towels. Place in a plastic bag, add flour and salt, and shake to coat well.

2 Heat a good drizzle of oil in a large, heavy-based fry pan. Cook shanks for a few minutes, turning to brown on all sides. Transfer to a casserole dish that the shanks can fit in snugly.

3 Wipe out fry pan with paper towels. Add a drizzle more oil and cook onion, carrot and garlic for 3–4 minutes or until soft. Add spices and pepper, and continue cooking for a further minute. Stir in cinnamon stick, tomato paste, crushed tomatoes, wine, stock and apricots.

4 Pour into casserole dish to just cover the shanks (if needed, add a little more stock to cover). Cover with a tight-fitting lid and cook in oven for about 3 hours, or until meat is tender and falling off the bone.

5 Mix all Lemon and Walnut Topping ingredients together in a small bowl and season with a little salt and pepper.

6 Sprinkle Lemon and Walnut Topping over lamb shanks just before serving. Serve with Lemon and Spinach Couscous or mashed potato and steamed greens (e.g. beans, spinach, broccoli, etc.).

ENERGY		CARBS	
2013kj / 482kcal		20g	
PROTEIN	**FAT**	**SAT FAT**	**SUGARS**
31.8g	26.5g	11.2g	15.4g

Corn, capsicum and bean rice

Pico de gallo

Mexican braised beef

Pink pickled red onions

MEXICAN FIESTA! Recipes over the page.

Mexican braised beef (or pork)

SERVES 4–6 **PREP TIME** 10 minutes **COOK TIME** 3½–4 hours   **DF | GF** (use GF soy sauce and GF beer or stock)

olive oil 1 tablespoon
onion 1, diced
smoked paprika 1 teaspoon
braising beef or pork (e.g. shoulder, brisket, chuck, blade, shin on the bone) 700–800g, cut into large 5cm chunks
chipotle sauce ¼ cup (see Note)
crushed tomatoes 400g can
brown sugar 1 tablespoon
soy sauce 1 tablespoon
dark beer (or beef or chicken stock) 1½ cups
dried chillies 1–3 (depending on how hot you like it!) or 1–2 teaspoons chilli flakes

Note

Find chipotle sauce (a smoked Mexican chilli sauce) in the sauces or international foods section of the supermarket.

Hola! It's a Mexican fiesta! One of the best ways to feed a crowd — it's tasty, colourful, fun, vibrant, and can get a little messy. All you need is some Latin music to dance to and plenty of sangria and you have one hell of a delicious party! Serve with some tacos if you want food that everyone can easily hold in their hands. Beef or pork works equally well, as does beans (use a combination of different dried beans) for a vegetarian version.

1 Preheat oven to 150°C. Heat olive oil in a heavy-based flameproof, ovenproof casserole dish or Dutch oven, or a fry pan. Cook onion until soft and starting to caramelise, 3–4 minutes. If you use a fry pan, transfer to a casserole dish with a tight-fitting lid.

2 Add smoked paprika, beef or pork, chipotle sauce, tomatoes, brown sugar, soy sauce, beer (or stock) and dried chillies. There should be just enough liquid to cover the meat — if there isn't, top it up with a little more beer or stock. Stir, cover with a tight-fitting lid and braise in oven for 3½–4 hours until meat is soft and shreds easily. Check on the meat after about 2 hours and top it up with a little more beer or stock if it looks like it is drying out.

3 Remove meat from the sauce and use two forks to roughly shred half of it (it's nice to leave some in chunks). Boil the sauce (in the dish it was cooked in or in a pot) on the stovetop for about 5 minutes or until it thickens. Return meat to the dish and mix together.

4 Serve with Pico de Gallo, Guacamole, Pink Pickled Red Onions, sour cream and One-pot Corn, Capsicum and Bean Rice and/or tacos or tortillas.

ENERGY	CARBS	PROTEIN	FAT	SAT FAT	SUGARS
1422kj / 340kcal	7.5g	31.1g	20.7g	8.5g	6.9g

Fill me up

One-pot corn, capsicum and bean rice

SERVES 6–8 **PREP TIME** 10 minutes
COOK TIME 30 minutes

DF | GF

A colourful, tasty side dish for any South American feast!

oil for cooking
onion 1, diced
red capsicum 1 large, cored, diced
corn kernels of 2 cobs (or 300g can corn kernels, drained)
smoked paprika ½ teaspoon
tomato purée 400g can (or a can of tomatoes, blitzed)
chicken or vegetable stock ¾ cup
long grain rice 1½ cups
salt ¾ teaspoon
canned beans (e.g. black beans or kidney beans) 400g can, rinsed and drained
coriander, chopped, ½ cup

1 Heat a good drizzle of oil in a large pot on medium heat. Cook onion, capsicum and corn for about 5 minutes until soft. Add paprika and continue to cook for a further 1–2 minutes.

2 Stir in tomato purée, stock, rice and salt. Cover with a tight-fitting lid and bring to the boil. As soon as it boils, reduce to low heat and cook, covered, for 18 minutes. Turn off heat and leave to steam, still covered, for a further 10 minutes.

3 Fluff up rice with a fork and toss with beans. Sprinkle over coriander just before serving.

ENERGY	CARBS		
1086kj / 256kcal	55.4g		
PROTEIN	**FAT**	**SAT FAT**	**SUGARS**
7.9g	0.8g	0g	4.3g

Pico de gallo (tomato, onion, coriander and jalapeño salsa)

MAKES 3–4 cups

DF | GF

This fresh salsa adds a big burst of flavour! I think the jalapeños are key, so if you can tolerate a bit of heat, make sure you add them!

Mix together 6-8 **vine-ripened tomatoes**, diced, 1 **Lebanese cucumber** (or ½ telegraph cucumber), diced, ¼ cup finely diced **red onion**, ¼ cup chopped **pickled jalapeños** (from a jar), juice of ½ **lemon**, drizzle of **extra-virgin olive oil**, ½ cup chopped **coriander** (leaves and stalks) and season to taste with **salt**.

Guacamole

DF | GF

In a bowl, roughly mash the flesh of 2 large just-ripe **avocados** and juice of ½ **lemon**. Season to taste with **salt** and **pepper**.

Pink pickled red onions

DF | GF

A very useful quick pickle that goes with lots of different dishes

In a medium bowl, mix ¼ cup **red wine vinegar** with 1 teaspoon **sugar**. Add 1 thinly sliced **red onion** and toss to combine. Leave to marinate for at least 30 minutes (or up to overnight) in the fridge.

Meatball bake with crunchy golden topping

SERVES 4–5 **PREP TIME** 20 minutes
COOK TIME 25 minutes

DF (use DF milk + omit cheeses)
GF (use GF breadcrumbs and bread)

MEATBALLS

breadcrumbs ⅓ cup
rosemary leaves, finely chopped,
2 teaspoons (or ¾ teaspoon dried herbs)
milk 3 tablespoons
onion ½, grated
beef mince 300–400g
raw pork sausage meat (squeezed out
of sausage casings) 300–400g
salt ¾ teaspoon
olive oil for cooking

TOMATO AND SPINACH SAUCE

olive oil 2 tablespoons
onion 1, chopped
garlic 2 cloves, chopped
rosemary 1 sprig
thyme leaves, chopped, 1 tablespoon
tomato paste 2–3 tablespoons
crushed tomatoes 2 x 400g cans
spinach or baby spinach 200–300g,
chopped
salt and pepper

TOPPING

ciabatta or focaccia bread 3 slices,
cut or torn into 2–3cm chunks
extra-virgin olive oil
mozzarella, grated, 1 cup
parmesan, grated, 2–3 tablespoons
thyme leaves (or rosemary), finely
chopped, 2–3 teaspoons
basil leaves a handful, to garnish

ENERGY	CARBS
2193kj / 525kcal	25.2g

PROTEIN	FAT	SAT FAT	SUGARS
49.2g	24.4g	9.8g	10.9g

This meatball bake has become a regular in our house now that my son Bodhi is around — he LOVES it (as his tomato sauce-stained face and hands show), as do most kids. To make these meatballs super tasty and juicy, I like to use half beef mince and half sausage meat — which you can either buy as is, or buy sausages and squeeze the meat out of the casings. The result of the dish relies on the quality of the sausages used, so get good-quality ones!

1 Preheat oven to 220°C. To make the meatballs, mix breadcrumbs, rosemary, milk and onion in a large mixing bowl and leave for a few minutes for breadcrumbs to soften. Add minces and salt and, using clean hands, mix everything together until well combined. Roll into walnut-sized balls and set aside on a plate.

2 Heat a good drizzle of olive oil in a large non-stick fry pan on medium-high heat. Brown meatballs all over for a few minutes, shaking the pan frequently, but do not cook all the way through — they should just be a little browned on the outside. Arrange meatballs in a large baking dish. Keep the pan on the heat.

3 To make the Tomato and Spinach Sauce, add olive oil to the pan and cook onion for 3–4 minutes until soft. Add garlic, rosemary sprig (keep it whole to just subtly flavour the sauce) and thyme, and continue to cook for a further 1–2 minutes. Add tomato paste, crushed tomatoes and spinach. Simmer for 5–10 minutes or until sauce has thickened slightly and greens are wilted. Season to taste with salt and pepper.

4 Pour sauce over meatballs, covering evenly. Arrange chunks of bread on top, drizzle with olive oil, and scatter with mozzarella, parmesan and thyme. Bake for about 15 minutes until bread is lightly toasted and cheese is melted and bubbly. Garnish with basil. Serve with steamed green veges or salad, and pasta or mashed potatoes.

Real Malaysian satay

MAKES 30 satay skewers (enough to serve 6) **PREP TIME** 40 minutes **COOK TIME** 20 minutes   **DF | GF**

MARINADE
lemongrass 3 stalks, chopped
garlic 3 cloves, peeled
fresh ginger 2cm piece, peeled and chopped
ground turmeric 2 teaspoons
brown sugar 1½ tablespoons
salt 1 teaspoon
oil 1½ tablespoons

SATAY
beef or lamb 500g (e.g. scotch, rump, sirloin), cut into bite-sized pieces
chicken thighs (boneless, skinless) 500g, cut into bite-sized pieces
bamboo skewers 30, soaked in water

PEANUT SAUCE
lemongrass 2 stalks, chopped
fresh ginger 3cm piece, peeled and chopped
ground cumin ½ teaspoon
ground coriander ½ teaspoon
chilli sauce 1–2 tablespoons (or 1 large chilli, finely chopped)
oil 2 tablespoons
lightly roasted peanuts 1 cup, coarsely ground in a blender or food processor, or very finely chopped
water ½ cup
tamarind juice 3–4 tablespoons (or 2 tablespoons lime or lemon juice) (see Tip page 50)
brown sugar 2–3 tablespoons
salt

Being half Malaysian, I know this satay is the real deal with its authentic marinade and peanut sauce (the key is using peanuts, not peanut butter!). Perfect for a barbecue, the smell you get when cooking these marinated meat skewers will have everyone salivating.

1 Place all marinade ingredients in a food processor and blend until a smooth paste. Alternatively, use a mortar and pestle to bash all the ingredients, except oil, together, then mix in oil.

2 Place chicken and beef or lamb pieces in separate bowls and stir the marinade through each. Leave to marinate in the fridge for at least 1 hour or overnight.

3 Thread marinated chicken and beef or lamb onto bamboo skewers and set aside until ready to cook.

4 To make the peanut sauce, combine lemongrass, ginger, cumin, coriander and chilli sauce (or chilli) in a food processor and blend until smooth. Alternatively, use a mortar and pestle to bash all the ingredients together to a paste. Heat oil in a wok and fry the spice paste for a few minutes until fragrant. Add peanuts, water, tamarind juice and sugar. Season with salt and simmer until thick, about 5 minutes.

5 Cook beef and chicken skewers on a preheated barbecue or grill plate until cooked through, about 3 minutes each side.

6 Serve with Peanut Sauce and some chopped cucumber and red onion.

 Tip

Buy fresh lemongrass from the herb section of the supermarket. Or, to save money, I buy frozen lemongrass stalks from the Asian supermarket which are really cheap! Alternatively you can buy pre-chopped lemongrass sold in jars at the supermarket in the international section.

ENERGY	CARBS	PROTEIN	FAT	SAT FAT	SUGARS
1804kj / 432kcal	18.8g	34g	25g	6.4g	8.4g
(per 4–5 skewers)					

Cauliflower cheese carbonara

SERVES 4–6 **PREP TIME** 15–20 minutes **COOK TIME** 15 minutes

CREAM SAUCE
cream ⅔ cup
free-range egg yolks 2
parmesan (or tasty cheddar cheese), finely grated, ½ cup + extra to serve
lemon zest and juice of ½
salt and pepper

GARLIC CRUMBS
butter 15g
garlic 2 cloves, finely chopped
breadcrumbs ½ cup (I used panko breadcrumbs)
thyme, finely chopped, 1 tablespoon
salt
parsley, finely chopped, ¼–½ cup

CAULIFLOWER CHEESE CARBONARA
dried fettuccine (or spaghetti) 360–400g
frozen peas 1 cup, defrosted
olive oil for cooking
bacon (or ham) 250g, rind removed, diced
onion, 1, finely diced
cauliflower ½–¾ head, cut into florets then thinly sliced
baby spinach 100–120g, chopped
salt and freshly ground black pepper

As a kid once said of this dish, 'Mum, it's like Cauliflower Cheese and Fettuccine Carbonara got married.' And that's a pretty perfect description of what to expect with this recipe, which combines two of my favourite childhood comfort foods. The kids will LOVE this one — and they'll be eating four different vegetables! Use spaghetti or any other type of pasta if you don't have fettuccine.

1 Bring a large pot of salted water to the boil.

2 To make the Cream Sauce, whisk cream, egg yolks, cheese, lemon zest and juice together in a large bowl. Season with salt and pepper. Set aside.

3 To make the Garlic Crumbs, melt butter in a large fry pan over medium heat. Add garlic, breadcrumbs and thyme, and cook, stirring frequently, for 1–2 minutes until golden and toasted. Season with a good pinch of salt. Remove from pan and set aside to cool, then mix with parsley.

4 Cook pasta in pot of boiling water for 8–10 minutes or until al dente (just cooked). Add peas for the last 1–2 minutes of cooking time. Scoop out ¼ cup of pasta water and reserve, then drain pasta and peas.

5 While pasta is cooking, heat a drizzle of oil in the same pan used for the crumbs on medium-high heat. Cook bacon and onion for 4–5 minutes. Remove from pan and set aside. Add a drizzle more oil and cook cauliflower for 2–3 minutes until golden. Leave in pan and remove from heat.

6 Working quickly, add hot pasta, peas, spinach, bacon and onion to fry pan with cauliflower. Pour in cream sauce and toss to coat (the residual heat from the pasta will be enough to cook the eggs and thicken the sauce). Add a few tablespoons of reserved pasta cooking water to loosen the sauce, if required. Check seasoning.

7 To serve, divide pasta and sauce between bowls and scatter with crumbs, and extra parmesan cheese if desired.

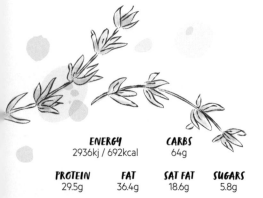

ENERGY	CARBS
2936kj / 692kcal	64g

PROTEIN	FAT	SAT FAT	SUGARS
29.5g	36.4g	18.6g	5.8g

Bacon, egg and mushroom picnic pie

SERVES 4–6 **PREP TIME** 15–20 minutes **COOK TIME** 30 minutes

shortcrust pastry 250g or 1½ square sheets
olive oil for cooking
bacon (e.g. streaky, middle eye, shoulder) 200g, roughly chopped
onion 1, chopped
mushrooms (e.g. Portobello or button) 150g, sliced (see Tip)
sour cream 150–200g, at room temperature
milk ¼ cup
free-range eggs 5
parmesan, (or tasty cheddar cheese) finely grated, ½ cup + extra to sprinkle on the top
thyme leaves, chopped, 1 tablespoon, (or ½ teaspoon dried mixed herbs)
salt and freshly ground black pepper a pinch
cherry tomatoes 200-250g, halved
parsley or basil pesto ¼ cup (or you could use tomato or fruit chutney)

Tips

• To avoid any moisture soaking into them, don't wash mushrooms. Instead, to clean them, simply use a pastry brush or paper towels to dust/wipe off any excess soil (don't forget, a little soil never hurt anyone anyway!).

• Pastry is easiest to work with when it's cold — if it's too warm, it can melt and be hard to shape and handle. If pastry is frozen, let it defrost on the bench or overnight in the fridge, and, once defrosted, store it in the fridge.

You don't have to be going on a picnic to eat this pie — though food tastes even better when you're outdoors. It's so delicious, and one of those versatile dishes that I'd happily eat for breakfast, lunch or dinner. Instead of bacon you can use ham, chorizo, or even replace the meat with some corn or diced capsicum for a vegetarian version.

1 Preheat an oven tray at 200°C. Roll out pastry on a lightly floured board or bench so that it is thinner and big enough to fit a 28cm (or thereabouts) pie dish, overhanging the edges a little. If using 1½ square sheets of pastry, join them together by slightly overlapping the edges. Don't bother trimming the edges — you'll fold any overhanging pastry over the top of the pie so it's nice and rustic, and we don't waste any pastry!

2 Heat a drizzle of oil in a large fry pan on medium heat. Cook bacon for a few minutes, then add onion and cook for a further 4–5 minutes until soft. Set aside. Add another drizzle of oil and mushrooms to the pan, and cook for about 5 minutes, until mushrooms are soft and all moisture from them has evaporated (the less moisture left in the pan, the better!).

3 In a large bowl, whisk sour cream with half of the milk until smooth, then add remaining milk, then eggs, cheese, thyme, salt and pepper and whisk together until smooth.

4 Scatter bacon, onion and mushrooms over pastry. Pour in egg mixture. Arrange cherry tomatoes (cut-side up) on top, dot with pesto or chutney, and sprinkle with extra cheese. Fold over any overhanging pastry and brush with a little milk or beaten egg. Place pie on the preheated oven tray and bake for about 30 minutes or until pastry is golden and filling is just set. Allow to sit in the pie dish for at least 15 minutes before cutting.

5 Serve with a leafy green salad, and some chutney (or good old T-sauce!) on the side.

ENERGY		CARBS	
2273kj / 536kcal		27.7g	
PROTEIN	**FAT**	**SAT FAT**	**SUGARS**
22.6g	38.4g	15.8g	4.2g

Wholegrain quinoa pizza base

MAKES 4 pizza bases
PREP TIME 15 minutes + 40 minutes to rise   **DF**

My original pizza base recipe rocks, but I like it even better with quinoa added — it makes it a bit more crispy, and it looks cool! If you just want a plain pizza base, omit the quinoa and replace with another 100g highgrade flour.

warm water 1 cup
active dried yeast 1 tablespoon
sugar 1 teaspoon
high-grade flour 350g
cooked quinoa 1 cup (150g)
olive oil 1 tablespoon
salt 1 teaspoon

1 Pour water into a mixing bowl and add yeast and sugar. Stir gently. Stand in a warm place for about 10 minutes until the mixture is frothy. Mix well.

2 Place the flour, cooked quinoa, olive oil and salt in a large mixing bowl. Add the yeast mixture and mix well to form a dough. (Note: there may be some leftover flour in the bowl once you've formed the dough, this is fine. Or the dough may feel too sticky, in which case, add a little more flour to it.)

3 Knead the dough for 10 minutes until smooth and elastic, then place in an oiled bowl (so it doesn't stick). Cover with a tea towel or clingfilm and leave in a warm place to rise until doubled in size (about 40 minutes).

4 Once it has risen, tip out onto a bench and divide into four even pieces. On a floured surface, roll out each piece into a disc about 20cm in diameter. Your pizza bases are now ready!

Speedy tomato sauce

COOK TIME 10 minutes   **DF | GF**

The speediest tomato pizza sauce recipe ever!

olive oil 1 tablespoon
crushed tomatoes 400g can
tomato paste 2 tablespoons
sugar 1 teaspoon
dried mixed herbs (or oregano) ½ teaspoon
salt and pepper

1 Stir all ingredients (except salt and pepper) together in a pan over medium heat and simmer, uncovered, for about 10 minutes, stirring frequently, until sauce is thick and the consistency of chutney.

2 Season to taste with salt and pepper. Allow to cool before using.

Storage

Pizza base dough (un-rolled and wrapped in clingfilm) will keep in the fridge for 2 days or can be frozen for up to 3–4 weeks. Defrost on the bench before using.

Pizza supreme

MAKES 4 pizzas, enough to serve 4–6 **PREP TIME** 15 minutes **COOK TIME** 12–15 minutes

pizza bases 4 (page 84)
Speedy Tomato Sauce 1 cup (page 84)
salami about 30 slices
button mushrooms 150g, sliced
red capsicum 1, cored, thinly sliced
green capsicum 1, cored, thinly sliced
cherry tomatoes 1 punnet (about 250g), cut in half
mozzarella, grated, 2–3 cups
parmesan, grated, ½ cup
basil leaves a handful

We love a good pizza in our house, and I'm not talking the greasy, floppy takeaway kind. A proper pizza with a thin, crispy base, home-made tomato sauce, fresh ingredient toppings and melted stringy cheese is one of my top go-to meals for a weekend night in for just Carlos and I, or for a casual dinner when we have friends around.

1 Preheat oven to 230°C. If you have one, place a pizza stone in the oven to preheat. Alternatively preheat an oven tray. Get it really hot (this helps the bases crisp up on the bottom).

2 Place one pizza base on a sheet of baking paper (so that you can lift the pizza easily once the toppings are on). Spread ¼ cup tomato sauce over base and arrange salami, mushrooms, capsicum and cherry tomatoes on top. Sprinkle with mozzarella and parmesan.

3 Carefully transfer the pizza (with baking paper) to hot pizza stone or oven tray. Cook for about 12 minutes or until pizza base is crisp and cheese has melted. Meanwhile get next pizza ready for the oven so it can go straight in after the first one comes out. Scatter fresh basil leaves on top, slice, and serve immediately.

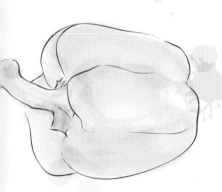

ENERGY	CARBS	PROTEIN	FAT	SAT FAT	SUGARS
2172kj / 520kcal	42.8g	28.5g	25.5g	11.4g	4.8g

Prosciutto and avocado pizza

MAKES 4 pizzas, enough to serve 4–6
PREP TIME 15 minutes **COOK TIME** 12–15 minutes

Here are another couple of my favourite pizza combinations.

pizza bases 4 (page 84)
Speedy Tomato Sauce 1 cup (page 84)
cherry tomatoes 1 punnet (about 250g), cut in half
mozzarella, grated, 2–3 cups
parmesan, grated, ½ cup
sour cream or crème fraîche ⅓ cup
lemon juice 2–3 teaspoons
prosciutto 150–200g
avocados (just ripe) 2, sliced
red onion ½, thinly sliced
basil leaves a handful
freshly ground black pepper

1 Follow the instructions for Pizza Supreme, but only place sauce, cherry tomatoes, mozzarella and parmesan on pizza base before cooking.

2 Mix sour cream and lemon juice together and set aside.

3 Top cooked pizza with prosciutto, avocados and red onion. Drizzle over sour cream and garnish with fresh basil. Grind over a little black pepper.

ENERGY		CARBS	
2479kj / 593kcal		42.9g	

PROTEIN	FAT	SAT FAT	SUGARS
31.8g	31.8g	11.1g	4.8g

Smoked salmon, rocket and caper pizza with lemon crème

MAKES 4 pizzas, enough to serve 4–6
PREP TIME 15 minutes **COOK TIME** 12–15 minutes

pizza bases 4 (page 84)
Speedy Tomato Sauce 1 cup (page 84)
cherry tomatoes 1 punnet (about 250g), cut in half
mozzarella, grated, 2–3 cups
parmesan, grated, ½ cup
crème fraîche or sour cream ½ cup
lemon zest and juice of 1
horseradish paste 2–3 teaspoons, to taste (optional)
hot smoked salmon 200g
capers, chopped, 1–2 tablespoons
red onion ½, thinly sliced
rocket leaves 2 handfuls

1 Follow the instructions for Pizza Supreme, but only place sauce, cherry tomatoes, mozzarella and parmesan on pizza base before cooking.

2 Mix crème fraîche, lemon zest and juice and horseradish (if using) together and set aside.

3 Arrange flakes of salmon on top of cooked pizza, followed by capers, red onion and rocket. Finish with a drizzle of lemon crème over the top.

ENERGY		CARBS	
2133kj / 510kcal		42.8g	

PROTEIN	FAT	SAT FAT	SUGARS
30.7g	23.5g	12g	4.8g

Cheesy bean and vege quesadillas with jalapeño jam

SERVES 4–6 **PREP TIME** 20 minutes **COOK TIME** 20 minutes

GF (use corn tortillas)

oil 1 tablespoon
onion 1, finely diced
garlic 1 clove, finely chopped
red or yellow capsicum 1, cored, finely diced
courgette 1, finely diced
corn kernels ¾ cup, (fresh, frozen or canned and drained)
smoked paprika 1 teaspoon
ground cumin 1 teaspoon
tomato paste 1 tablespoon
black beans or kidney beans 400g can, rinsed and drained
chipotle sauce 3 tablespoons (see Note page 37)
salt and pepper, to season
corn tortillas (or wheat tortillas) 10 small
grated cheese (I like to use a mix of grated mozzarella and cheddar, but any grated cheese such as edam or colby is fine) 2½ cups

JALAPEÑO JAM
olive oil 1 tablespoon
crushed tomatoes 400g can
pickled jalapeños (from a jar) ¼ cup, chopped
honey or brown sugar 2 teaspoons
salt and pepper, to season

TO SERVE
chopped coriander or torn basil leaves
natural unsweetened yoghurt or sour cream
Guacamole (page 73)

Tip

You can add cooked shredded chicken, pork or beef to the quesadilla filling if you like.

Like tacos, quesadillas ('kay-sa-dee-yas') are fun, relaxed food for sharing with friends — ideally with a beer and warm sunshine! These ones are crammed with beans, veges and oozing with cheese. The jalapeño jam is the perfect sweet and spicy condiment to dip into.

1 Heat oil in a fry pan on medium heat. Cook onion until soft, 3–4 minutes. Add garlic, capsicum, courgette, corn, paprika and cumin and continue cooking for a further 1 minute. Add tomato paste and cook for another minute. Take off the heat and mix in beans and chipotle sauce. Use a fork to roughly crush everything together. Season to taste with salt and pepper.

2 Lay a tortilla on a clean dry surface. Sprinkle with about ¼ cup grated cheese, spoon about ⅔ cup bean mixture on top, and sprinkle over another ¼ cup grated cheese. Top with another tortilla and press down gently but firmly. Repeat for remaining tortillas and filling.

3 Heat a drizzle of oil in a large fry pan (preferably non-stick) on low-medium heat. Cook each quesadilla for 2–3 minutes on one side, until golden brown and slightly crispy on the outside and cheese is melted. Press down on the quesadilla with a fish slice while cooking to help flatten it and make sure the filling sticks. Carefully flip over and cook for a further 2 minutes until golden brown on the other side. Repeat with remaining quesadillas.

4 To make the Jalapeño Jam, mix all ingredients in a pot and simmer for 8–10 minutes until thick and jam-like. Season with salt and pepper.

5 To serve, cut each quesadilla into four and pile onto a large plate or wooden board. Sprinkle with coriander or basil. Serve with yoghurt or sour cream, and Guacamole and Jalapeño Jam on the side.

ENERGY	CARBS	PROTEIN	FAT	SAT FAT	SUGARS
2341kj / 560kcal	66.2g	28.7g	20g	8.5g	11.1g

Summer tomato and basil tarte Tatin

SERVES 3–4 as a light meal **PREP TIME** 15 minutes **COOK TIME** 25 minutes

This dish sings summer. Make it when cherry tomatoes are in season and cheap. A tarte Tatin is an upside-down tart, mostly known as a dessert made with apples, but you can make all kinds, including savoury ones like this. The tomatoes go all sweet and juicy when cooked in the pan and are tipped out onto a golden, puffy pastry base — it's quite exciting when you turn it out! With fresh basil and creamy feta and served with a crisp garden salad (and a glass of pinot gris), it's a perfect summer meal.

butter 15g
olive oil a drizzle
cherry tomatoes 500g (2 punnets), mixed colours if you can get them
salt and freshly ground black pepper
balsamic vinegar 1 tablespoon
brown sugar 1 tablespoon
rosemary (or thyme) a few sprigs
puff pastry 1 square sheet
soft feta (or goats cheese) 50–70g
basil leaves a handful

1 Preheat oven to 220°C. Melt butter and olive oil in a medium-sized, heavy-based, ovenproof fry pan on high heat. Add cherry tomatoes and cook over high heat for 4–5 minutes, shaking the pan gently every now and again, until tomatoes are slightly blistered on the outside (do not cook until they burst and leak out their juice, they should still retain their shape). The pan should be crowded with tomatoes (no gaps). Season with salt and freshly ground black pepper.

2 Mix balsamic vinegar and brown sugar together and pour over tomatoes in the pan. Allow balsamic to bubble for about 1 minute until it has reduced and there is no longer much liquid left in the pan. Scatter with rosemary (or thyme). Turn off the heat.

3 Trim the four corners of the pastry so you have a rough round shape (just a little bigger than the size of the pan). Place pastry on top of the tomatoes in the pan and tuck the edges down around the inside of the pan (you can do this with a fork) to enclose the tomatoes. Prick the top of the pastry with a fork a few times (to allow steam to escape while cooking). Place in hot oven to bake for 22–25 minutes or until pastry is puffed and golden. Remove from oven, let tart sit for a few minutes and run a knife around the edge to release the pastry from the pan.

4 To flip the tart out onto a plate, place a plate (face down) on top of the pan and use a tea towel to hold the pan and plate together (so you don't burn yourself) and flip it over in one smooth movement. The tart will fall out onto the plate — ta da! Scatter feta (or goats cheese) and basil over the tart.

5 Cut tart into wedges and serve with a leafy green salad.

ENERGY	CARBS	PROTEIN	FAT	SAT FAT	SUGARS
1165kj / 279kcal	22g	6.2g	18g	11.6g	6.9g

Haloumi and vegetable saagwala

Whenever I go to an Indian restaurant, it's hard to go past ordering a saagwala, the rich spinach sauce served with lamb, chicken or paneer (Indian cheese). Here is my home-made version using haloumi instead of paneer (as they are very similar). Of course, you can use paneer, if you have it. And you could even turn it into a chicken saagwala by using cubes of chicken thighs, browned in the pan, instead.

haloumi 200g, cut into 1.5cm cubes
curry powder 1½ teaspoons
oil 3–4 tablespoons
cauliflower florets, chopped into roughly 1cm pieces, 1½–2 cups
onions 2, finely chopped
ground cumin 1 tablespoon
ground chilli ½–1 teaspoon
ground cloves ¼ teaspoon
ground turmeric ½ teaspoon
garlic 3 cloves, minced
fresh ginger, grated, 2 tablespoons
spinach leaves 300g, chopped
green chilli ½–1 large, chopped
crushed tomatoes 400g can
lemon juice of 1
salt and pepper
cream (or coconut cream) 2–3 tablespoons

CUCUMBER RAITA
telegraph cucumber ½ large
mint leaves, chopped, ½ cup
natural unsweetened yoghurt 1 cup
lime juice of 1
salt

TO SERVE
naan bread, 4–5, warmed (or use rice for GF)

1 Dust haloumi cubes with curry powder. Heat a drizzle of oil in large fry pan on a medium heat. Cook haloumi cubes until golden, tossing around pan frequently. Set aside on a plate. Keep pan on the heat.

2 Add cauliflower and a drizzle of oil to pan. Cook for 1–2 minutes, until starting to colour. Remove from pan and set aside with cooked haloumi.

3 Add another drizzle of oil and onions to the pan and fry until deep golden (but do not let burn), about 5–6 minutes. Add a tablespoon or two of water if it looks like they are ever catching on the bottom of the pan and burning. Add spices, garlic and ginger and fry for a further 2 minutes.

4 While onions are cooking, wilt spinach by blanching in boiling water or steaming in microwave. Lightly squeeze out excess water with your hands, then purée with chilli, tomatoes, cooked onions and spices, using a blender, stick blender or food processor.

5 Add purée to the same pan that onions and cauliflower were cooked in and simmer on medium heat until heated through, 2–3 minutes. Season with lemon juice and salt and pepper to taste. Stir through cauliflower and haloumi.

6 While saagwala is cooking, prepare raita and warm naan bread. To make raita, grate cucumber and combine with remaining ingredients. Season with salt.

7 Just before serving, drizzle cream over curry. Serve with naan bread and Cucumber Raita.

ENERGY	CARBS		
2614kj / 625kcal	52.2g		

PROTEIN	FAT	SAT FAT	SUGARS
23.4g	34.3g	13.7g	14.4g

Butternut and kaffir lime dhal (lentil curry)

SERVES 4–5 **PREP TIME** 25 minutes **COOK TIME** 35 minutes   **DF** (omit yoghurt) | **GF**

---

oil 2 tablespoons
onion 1, diced
garlic 2 cloves, chopped
fresh ginger 3cm piece, peeled and grated
kaffir lime leaf 2 small or 1 large, tough central stem removed, finely sliced (optional)
ground cumin, ground coriander, ground turmeric, garam masala
1 teaspoon of each
coconut milk 400g can
tomato paste 3 tablespoons
water 2 cups
dried split red lentils 1 cup
butternut (or pumpkin) 500g, peeled and cut into 2cm pieces
tomatoes 3–4, roughly chopped
ground chilli ½ teaspoon (optional)
sugar 1 teaspoon
salt ½ teaspoon
spinach (or silverbeet) 120g, chopped (optional)
lemon juice of 1

TO SERVE
natural unsweetened yoghurt ¼ cup
coriander, chopped, ¼–½ cup
roasted cashew nuts, chopped, ⅓ cup (optional)

A dhal is a simple curry made with lentils, and it is a great vegetarian recipe to have up your sleeve. It's nourishing and comforting; I liken it to the vegetarian version of chicken soup. Most dhals are plain, but I've added pumpkin to bulk it out and add a lovely sweetness and, if you have it, kaffir lime leaf makes a deliciously fragrant addition.

1 Heat oil in a large fry pan or pot on medium heat. Cook onion for 4–5 minutes until golden. Add garlic, ginger and kaffir lime leaf (if using) and cook for 1 minute. Add another drizzle of oil and spices and cook for 1 minute until fragrant. Add about ¼–½ cup of the coconut milk and stir to prevent spices burning.

2 Stir in remaining coconut milk, tomato paste, water, lentils, butternut, tomatoes, chilli (if using), sugar and salt. Bring to the boil, then cover partially and reduce heat to a simmer and cook for about 25 minutes, or until lentils and butternut are soft. Stir a few times during cooking to make sure lentils don't stick to the bottom of the pan and burn. Add a little extra water if it looks like it is drying out too much.

3 If using spinach or silverbeet, stir it through at the end. Season with lemon juice and more salt to taste, if needed.

4 Garnish dhal with yoghurt, coriander and cashew nuts (if using), and serve with steamed rice and/or naan bread.

ENERGY	CARBS	PROTEIN	FAT	SAT FAT	SUGARS
1921kj / 646kcal	40.7g	15.6g	24.4g	14.1g	13.3g

Fast + Fresh

SUPER

FRESH, FAST, TASTY, AND GOOD ENOUGH AS A MEAL
ON THEIR OWN, OR AN EXTRA-SPECIAL SIDE

SALADS

Poached chicken, sesame and cucumber salad

SERVES 4 **PREP TIME** 25 minutes **COOK TIME** 20 minutes   **DF** | **GF** (use GF soy sauce and hoisin sauce)

SOY-POACHED CHICKEN
water 3 cups
star anise 2 whole
cinnamon stick 1 whole
soy sauce ¼ cup
white wine ¼ cup
sesame oil 1 tablespoon
fresh ginger 2.5cm, thinly sliced
red chilli ½, sliced lengthways
crushed peppercorns 1 teaspoon
chicken breast (boneless, skinless)
400–500g

SALAD
telegraph cucumber ½, halved
lengthways, thinly sliced
baby radishes 3–4, thinly sliced
spring onions 3, thinly sliced
cherry tomatoes 1 punnet (about
250g), halved
celery 3 stalks, thinly sliced
roasted peanuts ½ cup, chopped
toasted sesame seeds 3 tablespoons
baby spinach 1–2 handfuls
mint leaves, chopped, ½ cup
coriander, chopped, ½ cup

DRESSING
hoisin sauce (home-made page 136 or
store-bought) 3 tablespoons
soy sauce 1½ tablespoons
rice vinegar (or apple cider vinegar or
lemon or lime juice) 1½ tablespoons
sesame oil 1½ tablespoons
fresh ginger, grated, 1½ teaspoons

lime 1, cut into wedges, to serve
(optional)

Poaching chicken breast is a great way to cook chicken without having to add any fat, whilst subtly infusing it with flavour. You can leave the chicken in the poaching liquid in the fridge if you are making parts of this dish ahead of time.

1 Combine all poached chicken ingredients in a pot. Cover with a tight-fitting lid and bring to a gentle simmer. Then turn off the heat and leave the chicken in the poaching liquid, still covered, for 14–18 minutes (depending on the size of the chicken breasts). Do not lift the lid during this time (so you don't let the heat escape) — the residual heat of the liquid will cook the chicken through perfectly and keep it nice and moist.

2 Remove chicken from the poaching liquid and set aside to cool slightly before slicing. If it has not cooked all the way through, simply return it to the pot and simmer in the poaching liquid for a couple more minutes.

3 Meanwhile, prepare all the salad ingredients and mix dressing ingredients together.

4 To serve, toss salad with 2–3 tablespoons of the dressing and place on a plate. Thinly slice chicken breasts, place on top of salad and drizzle with remaining dressing. Squeeze a lime wedge over the chicken, if desired.

	ENERGY	CARBS
	1652kj / 395kcal	11.6g

PROTEIN	FAT	SAT FAT	SUGARS
33.3g	21.5g	3.8g	9.1g

Beetroot, spiced almond, date and feta salad

SERVES 4 or 6 as a side salad **PREP TIME** 20 minutes **COOK TIME** 25–30 minutes   **DF** (omit feta) I **GF**

This is one of my go-to salads, either for a light meal or as an extra-special side salad. It's got a Middle Eastern touch with the dates, feta and the almonds, which are coated in a spice mixture.

1 Preheat oven to 200°C. Line an oven tray with baking paper.

2 In a bowl, mix vinegar and sugar. Add onion and toss to coat. Set aside in the fridge to marinate for about 20–30 minutes while you prepare the rest of the salad.

3 Toss beetroot with a good drizzle of olive oil and season with salt and pepper on lined tray. Roast for 25–30 minutes or until tender.

4 Heat a drizzle of olive oil in a fry pan. Cook almonds and garlic for about 2 minutes until golden. Turn off heat and mix in sumac, paprika, chilli and a pinch of salt.

5 When ready to serve, drain red onion (reserve vinegar) and toss with salad leaves, roast beetroot, spiced almonds, dates and feta. Dress with extra-virgin olive oil and some reserved vinegar.

red wine vinegar 3 tablespoons
sugar 1 teaspoon
red onion ½, thinly sliced
beetroot (any colour e.g. red or yellow) 3 large or 4 medium, peeled and cut into 2–3cm cubes
olive oil a drizzle
salt and pepper
almonds, chopped, ½ cup
garlic 3 cloves, chopped
sumac 1 tablespoon (see Note page 46)
paprika ½ teaspoon
chilli flakes ½ teaspoon
baby spinach and/or baby beetroot leaves 120g
medjool dates 4–5 (or 6–8 dried dates), pitted, chopped
feta 75–100g, crumbled
extra-virgin olive oil for dressing

ENERGY	CARBS	PROTEIN	FAT	SAT FAT	SUGARS
953kj / 228kcal	17.4g	8.5g	12.6g	3.2g	16.3g

Bok choy slaw with steak and ponzu

SERVES 4 **PREP TIME** 20 minutes **COOK TIME** 5–10 minutes   **DF | GF** (use GF soy sauce)

oil for cooking
rump, sirloin or eye fillet steak 400g
salt

PONZU DRESSING
soy sauce or tamari 1 tablespoon
lemon juice of ½ (or 1 lime)
sesame oil 1 teaspoon
rice vinegar (or apple cider vinegar)
2 teaspoons
sweet chilli sauce 1½ teaspoons
fresh ginger, finely grated, 1 teaspoon
red chilli 1 large, finely chopped
(optional)
kaffir lime leaf 1, tough inner stem
removed, finely sliced (optional)

BOK CHOY SLAW
cabbage, shredded or finely sliced,
3 cups
baby bok choy 3–4, leaves and stems
finely sliced
celery 2 stalks, finely sliced
roasted peanuts, chopped, ¾ cup
coriander, chopped, ¾ cup
sesame seeds 2 tablespoons, lightly
toasted

It's a little-known fact (well, probably not for long now) that raw bok choy is fantastic in salads. It's crisp, fresh and crunchy, everything you want in a good slaw. Of course, you can also use more shredded cabbage instead, but do make sure you give the bok choy a go sometime — I reckon you'll love it.

1 Heat a drizzle of oil in a fry pan on medium-high heat. Pat steak dry with paper towels and season with salt. Cook for 2–3 minutes on each side for medium-rare, or until done to your liking. Set aside, covered with foil, to rest for 10 minutes.

2 While steak is resting, prepare the Bok Choy Slaw ingredients and mix all Ponzu Dressing ingredients together. Slice steak across the grain.

3 Toss all Bok Choy Slaw ingredients together and dress with Ponzu Dressing just before serving.

4 Serve slaw topped with slices of steak and drizzled with any remaining dressing.

Tip

Add cooked vermicelli noodles to make this a more substantial meal.

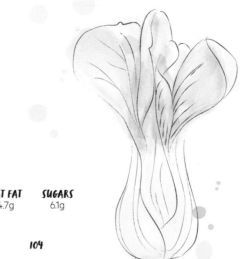

ENERGY	CARBS	PROTEIN	FAT	SAT FAT	SUGARS
1346kj / 322kcal	10.1g	27g	19.2g	4.7g	6.1g

Watermelon, avocado, cucumber and chilli salad

SERVES 4 or 6 as a side salad **PREP TIME** 20 minutes   **DF | GF**

Lebanese cucumbers 2
watermelon ½ large, skin removed, flesh
cut into roughly 3cm cubes
avocado (just ripe) 1 large, sliced
red or green chilli 1 large, deseeded,
finely chopped
lime, zest of 1 (or kaffir lime leaves, 2,
inner stem removed, finely sliced)
mint leaves 1 small handful
limes juice of 2
extra-virgin olive oil (or avocado oil)
flaky sea salt and **freshly ground black
pepper**

*I'm in love with this salad — it's so refreshing, with big
chunks of cooling watermelon and cucumber, creamy
avocado and, for those of us who like a bit of a kick, a little
chilli. It makes a great summer side, light meal or starter.
A crumbling of feta can also be a nice addition for a little
salty zing.*

1 Cut cucumbers in half lengthways, scoop out seeds with a
teaspoon, and slice.

2 On a large platter, toss cucumber, watermelon, avocado,
chilli, lime zest and mint together.

3 Squeeze over lime juice and drizzle with extra-virgin olive
oil (or avocado oil). Season with sea salt and black pepper.

ENERGY	CARBS	PROTEIN	FAT	SAT FAT	SUGARS
907kj / 217kcal	27.4g	3.0g	9.9g	1.3g	24.7g

Balsamic-glazed pumpkin, date and haloumi quinoa salad

SERVES 4 or 6 as a side salad **PREP TIME** 25–30 minutes **COOK TIME** 30 minutes

GF

ROAST PUMPKIN
pumpkin or butternut (skin on) 500g, cut into 2cm chunks
balsamic vinegar 2 tablespoons
olive oil 1 tablespoon
liquid honey 1 tablespoon

QUINOA SALAD
quinoa 1 cup
water 1½ cups
avocado (firm ripe) flesh of 2, sliced
cherry tomatoes 1 punnet (about 250g), halved
seedless grapes 1 cup, halved
medjool dates 6–8, stone removed, chopped
baby spinach or rocket 1 handful
flat-leaf parsley, chopped, ¾ cup
salt and pepper

olive oil for cooking
haloumi 200g, sliced 0.5cm thick

DRESSING
red wine vinegar 3 tablespoons
wholegrain mustard 1 tablespoon
lemon juice of 1
liquid honey 1 tablespoon
extra-virgin olive oil 3 tablespoons

One of my favourite vegetarian meals — hearty and filling enough to have as a meal on its own, but it would also make a fantastic extra-special side.

1 Preheat oven to 200°C. Line an oven tray with baking paper.

2 Toss pumpkin with balsamic vinegar, olive oil and honey in prepared tray. Roast until slightly caramelised, 20–25 minutes.

3 Meanwhile, cook the quinoa. Combine quinoa and water (with a pinch of salt) in a medium-sized pot and bring to the boil. As soon as it boils, cover with a tight-fitting lid and reduce to lowest heat to cook for 15 minutes. Remove from heat and leave to steam, still covered, for 10 minutes.

4 Fluff up quinoa grains with a fork and toss with roast pumpkin and remaining quinoa salad ingredients. Season to taste with salt and pepper.

5 Heat a drizzle of oil in a fry pan on medium heat and cook haloumi slices for 1–2 minutes on each side until golden brown, and melted on the inside. Mix all dressing ingredients together and toss with quinoa salad.

6 To serve, divide Quinoa Salad between bowls and top with slices of cooked haloumi.

ENERGY	CARBS	PROTEIN	FAT	SAT FAT	SUGARS
2740kj / 655kcal	48.7g	17.5g	42g	11.3g	27.4g

Grilled peach, crispy bacon and haloumi salad

SERVES 4 or 6 as a side salad **PREP TIME** 15 minutes **COOK TIME** 10 minutes   **GF**

This mouth-watering salad is perfection. Make it in the peak of summer when peaches (or nectarines) are at their sweetest and juiciest. Grilling brings out all those lovely fruity sweet flavours, perfectly complemented by salty bacon and haloumi.

1 In a bowl, mix vinegar and sugar together. Add red onion and toss with vinegar mixture. Set aside to marinate for about 20 minutes while you prepare the rest of the salad.

2 Heat a drizzle of oil on the barbecue hot plate or in a fry pan or grill pan on the stovetop. Cook bacon until crispy; set aside. Cook peaches (in the bacon fat) for a couple of minutes each side until nicely caramelised; set aside.

3 Pat haloumi dry with paper towels, then cook for 1–2 minutes on each side until golden.

4 Arrange salad leaves on a large serving platter. Arrange grilled peaches, bacon and haloumi slices on top. Drain red onion, reserving the vinegar, and scatter on top.

5 Mix reserved red wine vinegar with remaining dressing ingredients and dress salad just before serving.

red wine vinegar 2 tablespoons
sugar 1 teaspoon
red onion ½, thinly sliced
oil for cooking
bacon 4 rashers (up to you what cut you use, I used streaky), diced
peaches (ripe) 3, stones removed, cut into 6–8 wedges each (nectarines would be delish too!)
haloumi 200g, sliced about 1cm-thick
mixed salad leaves 4–6 large handfuls

DRESSING
liquid honey 2 teaspoons
extra-virgin olive oil 2 tablespoons
wholegrain mustard 1 teaspoon

ENERGY	CARBS	PROTEIN	FAT	SAT FAT	SUGARS
1405kj / 336kcal	10.7g	15.5g	25.5g	11.2g	10.5g

Roast roots, bacon, walnut and orange salad

SERVES 4 or 6 as a side salad **PREP TIME** 15 minutes **COOK TIME** 30–35 minutes   **DF | GF**

I love a warm roast vegetable salad and this one ticks all the boxes: sweet caramelised roast root vegetables, crispy bacon, freshness from orange and rocket (or any other leafy green you like) and a scattering of toasted nuts, with a perfectly balanced honey mustard dressing. It's hearty and filling enough to have as a meal on its own, but also makes a fabulous special side salad.

SALAD
red kumara (skin on) 300g, cut into 2–3cm chunks
baby parsnips (skin on) 300g, scrubbed and cut in half lengthways (or large parsnips, sliced 1-2cm thick on an angle)
baby carrots 300g, scrubbed and cut in half lengthways (or large carrots, sliced 1-2cm thick on an angle)
liquid honey 2 teaspoons
olive oil a drizzle
salt and pepper
streaky bacon 4–6 rashers, diced
walnuts, chopped, ½ cup
rocket leaves 4 handfuls
oranges 2, skin removed, sliced

HONEY MUSTARD DRESSING
wholegrain mustard 2 teaspoons
liquid honey 2 teaspoons
lemon juice of 1
extra-virgin olive oil 2 tablespoons
salt and pepper

1 Preheat oven to 200°C. Line an oven tray with baking paper.

2 Toss kumara, parsnips and carrots with honey and a good drizzle of olive oil in lined roasting tray. Season with salt and pepper, and roast for 30–35 minutes or until tender and slightly caramelised.

3 Heat a drizzle of oil in a fry pan, and fry bacon until crispy. Set aside on paper towels to drain. Keep pan on heat and lightly toast walnuts for 2–3 minutes.

4 Mix all dressing ingredients together and season to taste with salt and pepper.

5 To serve, toss roast vegetables, rocket, orange, crispy bacon and walnuts with Honey Mustard Dressing and divide between plates.

ENERGY	CARBS	PROTEIN	FAT	SAT FAT	SUGARS
1758kj / 420kcal	33.8g	12.7g	24.9g	6.4g	19.1g

Autumn harvest salad

SERVES 4 or 6 as a side salad **PREP TIME** 20 minutes **COOK TIME** 25–35 minutes   **GF**

pumpkin or butternut (skin on) 800g–1kg, cut into 2cm pieces
olive oil 1 tablespoon
maple syrup or liquid honey 1 tablespoon
salt and **freshly ground black pepper**
walnuts, chopped, ¾ cup
butter large knob
sage leaves ⅓ cup, washed and dried with paper towels
salad leaves (e.g. baby rocket or spinach) 4 handfuls
pears (just-ripe) 2 medium or 3 small, sliced
medjool dates 6–8, pitted, chopped
feta 100g

HONEY BALSAMIC MUSTARD DRESSING
balsamic vinegar 1½ tablespoons
liquid honey 2 teaspoons
extra-virgin olive oil 1½ tablespoons
wholegrain mustard 1 teaspoon

This salad is full of the best of autumn's bounty, with caramelised roast butternut, crisp, sweet pear, toasted walnuts and buttery sage.

1 Preheat oven to 180°C. Line an oven tray with baking paper.

2 Toss butternut, olive oil and maple syrup in prepared oven tray. Season with salt and freshly ground black pepper. Roast for about 25–35 minutes or until soft, caramelised and golden.

3 Toast walnuts in a dry fry pan (no oil) on medium heat for 1–2 minutes. Set aside. Melt butter in fry pan and, when it starts to bubble, add sage leaves and fry for 1–2 minutes until crispy.

4 Mix all dressing ingredients together.

5 Just before serving, toss salad leaves with dressing and divide between plates. Arrange roast butternut, pear and dates on top. Scatter with walnuts and crumble feta on top. Lastly, top with fried sage leaves and drizzle with any remaining brown butter from the pan.

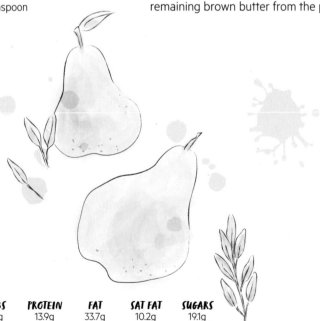

ENERGY	CARBS	PROTEIN	FAT	SAT FAT	SUGARS
2218kj / 530kcal	39.9g	13.9g	33.7g	10.2g	19.1g

Spiced haloumi and beetroot salad with fruity tamarillo dressing

SERVES 4 or 6 as a side salad **PREP TIME** 15 minutes **COOK TIME** 20 minutes   **GF**

MAPLE-ROAST BEETROOT
beetroot 4 medium-sized, cut into 3cm pieces (I leave the skin on)
maple syrup (or liquid honey)
1 tablespoon
olive oil 1 tablespoon
salt and pepper

TAMARILLO DRESSING
tamarillos flesh of 2 large, diced
Dijon mustard ½ teaspoon
liquid honey 1½ teaspoons
extra-virgin olive oil 1½ tablespoons

SPICED HALOUMI
ground cumin ½ teaspoon
ground turmeric ¼ teaspoon
salt ¼ teaspoon
haloumi 200g, cut into 0.5–1cm thick slices
olive oil for cooking

SALAD
rocket (or baby spinach leaves)
4 handfuls
sunflower seeds ¼ cup, toasted

In this salad, the tamarillos give the fruity tartness that all good dressings need. It goes great with roasted beetroot, especially when it's caramelised to intensify its natural earthy sweetness.

1 Preheat oven to 200°C. Line an oven tray with baking paper.

2 Toss beetroot with maple syrup (or honey) and olive oil in prepared tray. Season with salt and pepper and roast for about 20 minutes until beetroot is soft.

3 Mix all Tamarillo Dressing ingredients together and set aside for at least 10 minutes for the flavours to blend.

4 On a plate, mix cumin, turmeric and salt together. Lightly dust haloumi slices in spice mixture to lightly coat. Heat a drizzle of olive oil in a large non-stick fry pan on medium-high heat. Cook haloumi for 1–2 minutes on each side, or until golden outside and soft and melted inside.

5 To serve, divide rocket leaves between plates, top with roast beetroot, haloumi (straight from the hot pan) and sunflower seeds. Spoon Tamarillo Dressing on top.

Tip
You can use ¾ teaspoon curry powder as a substitute to the ground cumin and turmeric.

ENERGY	CARBS	PROTEIN	FAT	SAT FAT	SUGARS
1587kj / 379kcal	16.3g	16.3g	26.6g	10.1g	14.7g

Sticky chilli and lime chicken, corn and avocado salad

SERVES 4 **PREP TIME** 20 minutes **COOK TIME** 20 minutes   **DF | GF** (use GF soy sauce)

Sticky Chilli Sauce 5 tablespoons (page 156 or a shop-bought sweet chilli sauce)
lime juice 3 tablespoons
garlic 2 cloves, minced
fish sauce or soy sauce
1½ tablespoons
chicken breasts (boneless, skinless) 600g
corn cobs 4, husk and silk removed
oil 1 tablespoon

TO SERVE
baby cos lettuces 2, roughly chopped
avocados (just-ripe) 2, sliced
cherry tomatoes 1 punnet (about 250g), halved
spring onions 2, finely sliced
coriander, chopped, ½ cup + extra to garnish
extra-virgin olive or avocado oil drizzle of
limes 2, halved, to serve

A quick and easy chicken salad is a must-have recipe for your repertoire: it's the perfect meal for a weeknight, weekend barbecue, or lunch — and it's a winner with every family member. The grilled chicken gets tossed and coated in my Sticky Chilli Sauce, making it extra delicious.

1 Combine Sticky Chilli Sauce, lime juice, garlic and fish or soy sauce in a small bowl.

2 Pat chicken dry with paper towels and cut in half, horizontally, to form flat-ish steaks. Set aside.

3 Preheat barbecue or a large fry pan on medium-high heat. Brush corn cobs with oil and cook for about 10 minutes, turning frequently, until golden. Set aside to cool while you cook the chicken.

4 Season chicken with salt. Cook chicken steaks for about 5 minutes each side until browned and just cooked through. Set aside to rest for a few minutes, then slice. Return pan to the heat and add the chilli sauce mixture and cook until bubbling and beginning to become jammy. Turn off the heat. Return sliced chicken to the pan and toss in glaze to coat.

5 Cut kernels off corn cobs, trying to keep the kernels in big chunks. Toss lettuce, avocado, corn, tomatoes, spring onion and coriander with extra-virgin olive or avocado oil and divide between plates. Top with chicken and glaze, and squeeze over limes. Garnish with extra coriander.

ENERGY	CARBS	PROTEIN	FAT	SAT FAT	SUGARS
2195kj / 525kcal	21.7g	40.1g	30g	4.6g	14.7g

Charred broccoli and brown rice salad

SERVES 4 or 6 as a side salad **PREP TIME** 10 minutes **COOK TIME** 25 minutes   **DF | GF** (use GF soy sauce)

brown rice 1 cup
water 1½ cups
salt a good pinch
broccolini 2 bunches (about 300g), trimmed (or 2 small heads broccoli, cut into 1cm-thick slices)
oil 1 tablespoon
lemon juice of ½
garlic 1 clove, minced
Chinese five spice ¼ teaspoon
carrot 1 large, peeled and shredded or coarsely grated
roasted peanuts, chopped, ½ cup
red capsicum 1, cored and thinly sliced
avocado (firm ripe) 1 large, sliced
coriander (or flat-leaf parsley), chopped, ½ cup

DRESSING
soy sauce or tamari 2 tablespoons
lime juice of 1 (or ½ lemon)
sesame oil 1½ teaspoons
rice vinegar (or apple cider vinegar) 1 tablespoon
sweet chilli sauce 2 teaspoons
fresh ginger, finely grated, 1½ teaspoons

Barbecuing, grilling or roasting broccoli until the ends are a little brown and charred takes its flavour to a whole new level in this Asian-inspired salad. It helps to pat the broccoli dry with paper towels so that you get those nice charred ends and don't end up steaming it instead.

1 Place rice, water and salt in a medium-sized pot and bring to the boil. As soon as it boils, cover with a tight-fitting lid and reduce to low heat to cook for 15 minutes. Turn off heat and leave to steam, still covered, for 10 minutes. Do not remove lid at any time while rice is cooking and steaming. Fluff up with a fork and set aside to cool (it works best if you can spread the rice out in a flat dish and leave it in the fridge or freezer for 15–30 minutes.

2 Preheat a large grill pan or fry pan (or the barbecue) over medium heat. In a large bowl, toss broccolini with oil, lemon juice, garlic, five spice and a pinch of salt to coat. Grill broccolini for a few minutes on each side or until lightly charred and just tender (but still has some crunch).

3 Mix all dressing ingredients together. Toss cooled rice with charred broccoli, carrot, peanuts, capsicum, avocado, coriander and dressing just before serving.

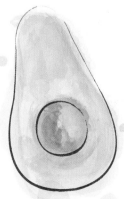

ENERGY	CARBS	PROTEIN	FAT	SAT FAT	SUGARS
2140kj / 512kcal	45.5g	17.3g	27.3g	4g	6.9g

Asparagus, kumara, walnut and parmesan salad

SERVES 4–6 **PREP TIME** 20 minutes **COOK TIME** 25 minutes   **DF** (omit parmesan) | **GF**

If asparagus isn't in season you could use green beans instead.

kumara (skin on) 400–500g, cut into 3cm chunks
olive oil a drizzle
salt and pepper
red wine vinegar 2 tablespoons
sugar 1 teaspoon
red onion ½, thinly sliced
asparagus (or green beans) 250g, trimmed
flat-leaf parsley, chopped, ¼ cup
lightly toasted walnuts, chopped, ⅓ cup
parmesan shaved, ¼ cup

HONEY MUSTARD DRESSING
wholegrain mustard 2 teaspoons
liquid honey 2 teaspoons
extra-virgin olive oil 2 tablespoons
reserved red wine vinegar (from the pickled onion) 1 tablespoon

1 Preheat oven to 200°C. Line an oven tray with baking paper. Toss kumara with a good drizzle of olive oil on prepared tray, season with salt and pepper, and roast for about 25 minutes or until golden and tender.

2 In a bowl, mix red wine vinegar and sugar together and add red onion. Leave to marinate for about 15 minutes. Drain, reserving vinegar for the dressing.

3 Place asparagus in a pot or heatproof dish or bowl, and pour over boiling water to cover. Leave to stand for 5–10 minutes until asparagus is lightly cooked through (but still crunchy). Drain and place in a bowl of iced water to quickly cool (this helps it retain its bright green colour) then drain again.

4 Mix all dressing ingredients together.

5 Toss roast kumara, asparagus, parsley, walnuts, and half of dressing, pickled red onion and parmesan together. Scatter over remaining pickled red onion and parmesan, and drizzle with remaining dressing.

ENERGY	CARBS	PROTEIN	FAT	SAT FAT	SUGARS
1208kj / 289kcal	28.6g	8.2g	15.1g	2.8g	8.9g

Share around

SIDES & NIBBLY THINGS.

SIMPLE SIDES TO COMPLETE THE PERFECT MEAL AND TASTY TIDBITS TO HAND AROUND

Golden courgette fries

ground almonds ½ cup
parmesan, very finely grated (use a microplane or the finest side of the grater), ½ cup
thyme or rosemary, very finely chopped, 1½ tablespoons
herb salt (or normal salt) ½ teaspoon
free-range egg 1, lightly beaten
courgettes 3 medium (try to get straight, not-too-bendy ones)

AÏOLI
mayonnaise 2–3 tablespoons
natural unsweetened yoghurt
2 tablespoons
garlic ½ small clove, minced
lemon finely grated zest of ½
lemon juice 1 tablespoon
smoked paprika ¼ teaspoon
salt and freshly ground black pepper

These 'fries' are very addictive and moreish but, hey, when you're actually eating green vegetables, I say it's okay to eat a whole bowl! They crisp up on the outside and are scrumptious served with aïoli to dip into. They're a nice change to potato fries, and a clever way to get everyone eating their green veges — they'll get gobbled up quickly though, so a second batch will almost always be required.

1 Preheat oven to 220°C. Line a baking tray with baking paper.

2 Mix ground almonds, parmesan, herbs and salt in a bowl. Beat egg in a separate bowl.

3 Trim the top and bottom off the courgettes, then cut each courgette in half. Cut each piece of courgette into quarters lengthways, then cut out the core to remove the seeds (they can be a little too watery). Cut each piece into 1cm-thick fingers, just like chips.

4 Dip each courgette finger in beaten egg and then in crumb mixture, making sure they are well coated. (To avoid a sticky mess, use one hand for the egg bowl and one hand for the crumb mixture bowl!) Arrange fries on prepared baking tray and bake for 12–15 minutes or until golden and crispy.

5 Mix all Aïoli ingredients together and season to taste with salt and freshly ground black pepper.

6 Serve courgette fries straight from the oven with Aïoli. Yum yum!

ENERGY	CARBS	PROTEIN	FAT	SAT FAT	SUGARS
999kj / 239kcal	5.2g	12.4g	19.2g	5.3g	2.7g

Smoky kumara and parsnip fries with sweet chilli yoghurt

SERVES 4
PREP TIME 10 minutes
COOK TIME 35–45 minutes

DF (without sweet chilli yoghurt) **| GF**

A drizzle of maple syrup really helps bring out the natural sweetness in the kumara and parsnip — so delicious combined with the smokiness of the paprika. Great as a healthy nibble and a side to so many dishes.

orange kumara 300g, scrubbed (leave skin on)
parsnips 300g, scrubbed (leave skin on)
olive oil 2 tablespoons
maple syrup 1 tablespoon
smoked paprika ½– ¾ teaspoon
ground chilli (or cayenne pepper) ⅛–¼ teaspoon (optional)
herb salt (or normal salt) ½ teaspoon

SWEET CHILLI YOGHURT
natural Greek yoghurt (or sour cream) ¼ cup
sweet chilli sauce 2 teaspoons

1 Preheat oven to 220°C. Line a large oven tray with baking paper.

2 Cut kumara and parsnips into 1cm-thick wedges or chips. Toss with olive oil, maple syrup, paprika, chilli and herb salt in the prepared oven tray. (Make sure kumara and parsnip are in a single layer.) Roast for 35–45 minutes or until golden and crispy. Turn once or twice during cooking.

3 Mix Sweet Chilli Yoghurt ingredients together and serve with the fries.

ENERGY	CARBS		
857kj / 205kcal	28.4g		
PROTEIN	**FAT**	**SAT FAT**	**SUGARS**
2.8g	8.3g	1.8g	18.4g

Iceberg wedge with creamy green dressing

SERVES 4
PREP TIME 10 minutes

DF | GF

I love the humble iceberg lettuce for its refreshing, cooling crunch and simplicity. Sometimes it's all you need as a side salad, with a really good dressing such as this creamy avocado one.

CREAMY GREEN DRESSING
lemon juice of 1
parsley (and/or basil or coriander), chopped, ⅓ cup
dill, chopped, 2 teaspoons
avocado (just ripe) flesh of 1
water ½ cup
salt and pepper

iceberg lettuce 1 large
chives, chopped, to garnish (optional)

1 Blitz all dressing ingredients in a blender and season to taste with salt and pepper (add a little more water as needed, to get the right consistency).

2 Remove the 1–2 outer leaves of the iceberg lettuce, then cut it into four wedges. Dress with Creamy Green Dressing and garnish with chives, if using.

ENERGY	CARBS		
517kj / 123kcal	1.9g		
PROTEIN	**FAT**	**SAT FAT**	**SUGARS**
2.1g	11.4g	1.6g	1.3g

Sweet roast capsicum, tomato, feta and basil salad

SERVES 4–6 **PREP TIME** 20 minutes **COOK TIME** 35–45 minutes   **GF**

---

red capsicums 3
yellow capsicums 3
cherry tomatoes 1 punnet
(about 250g), halved
feta 100g
basil leaves 1 cup
**flaky sea salt and freshly ground
  black pepper**
extra-virgin olive oil a good glug
lemon juice and zest of ½

Make this when capsicums are cheap and in-season. Roasting or grilling them (until charred and blistered) intensifies their natural flavour and sweetness, gives them a subtle smokiness, and are much nicer than the ones you buy in the jar. A great side dish for a barbecue.

1 Either preheat oven to 220°C, or preheat barbecue to high. Place whole capsicums in a roasting dish or on an oven tray, and roast in the oven for 35–45 minutes until charred and blistered. Alternatively, char whole capsicums on the barbecue for about 20 minutes, turning a few times, until charred and blistered. Set aside to cool, then peel off skins (they should come off easily), and slice flesh, discarding seeds.

2 Arrange tomatoes and roasted capsicum on a serving platter and scatter with crumbled feta and basil leaves. Season with flaky sea salt and freshly ground black pepper, and dress with extra-virgin olive oil, lemon juice and zest.

ENERGY	CARBS	PROTEIN	FAT	SAT FAT	SUGARS
364kj / 87kcal	5.8g	5g	4.6g	2.9g	5.4g

Broccoli, almond and cranberry salad

SERVES 4–6 **PREP TIME** 15 minutes **COOK TIME** 5 minutes   **GF**

broccoli 1 large or 2 small heads,
chopped into small florets
apple (e.g. Braeburn or Granny Smith)
1, cored
lemon juice of 1
almonds, sliced, slivered or chopped,
⅓ cup
dried cranberries, chopped, ¼ cup
spring onions 2, finely sliced

DRESSING
natural yoghurt ¼ cup
mayonnaise 2 tablespoons
apple cider vinegar 1 teaspoon
liquid honey ½ teaspoon
salt and pepper

*Very lightly cooked, almost raw broccoli (so that it's got
a good amount of crunch), makes a great salad with
almonds, cranberries, fresh apple and a light creamy
dressing.*

1 Place broccoli florets in a large heatproof bowl and pour
over boiling water to cover. Leave for 5 minutes or so to
lightly cook. Meanwhile, get a large bowl of iced water
ready. Drain broccoli and place in bowl of iced water (this
helps the broccoli retain its bright green colour and
crunchiness).

2 Thinly slice apple, then cut into thin matchsticks and
place in the bowl the broccoli was cooked in. Squeeze
lemon juice over the apple to prevent browning. Lightly
toast almonds in a dry fry pan (no oil) on medium heat,
shaking the pan frequently to avoid burning, for
2–3 minutes, until light golden.

3 Mix dressing ingredients together and season with salt
and pepper.

4 Drain broccoli well and toss with apple, cranberries,
spring onion and half of the dressing. Drizzle with
remaining dressing and scatter almonds on top.

Tip
For extra flavour,
add some cooked
diced crispy bacon
to the salad!

ENERGY	CARBS	PROTEIN	FAT	SAT FAT	SUGARS
902kj / 215kcal	12.9g	6.5g	14.5g	2.5g	12.3g

Spinach, cucumber and radish with Japanese sesame dressing

SERVES 4–6 **PREP TIME** 10 minutes **COOK TIME** 3 minutes

DF | GF (use GF soy sauce)

JAPANESE SESAME DRESSING
sesame seeds 1½ tablespoons
mayonnaise 2½ tablespoons
rice vinegar 1 tablespoon
soy sauce 1½ tablespoons
sugar 1 teaspoon
sesame oil ½ teaspoon

SALAD
baby spinach 4–6 handfuls
Lebanese cucumbers 2 (or ½ telegraph cucumber), cut in half lengthways, seeds scraped out with a teaspoon and sliced
baby radishes 3–4, thinly sliced
avocado (firm ripe) 1, sliced (optional)

*This salad is all about the dressing. If you've ever had **that** Japanese sesame dressing (called goma dressing) you'll know how delicious it is, and you've probably wondered 'how do they make it?'. I've finally cracked the recipe after trying to replicate it many times and this is better than the bought stuff (and without the additives)!*

1 Toast sesame seeds in a dry fry pan (no oil), moving around the pan frequently, for a few minutes until light golden. Crush 1 tablespoon of sesame seeds to a paste in a mortar and pestle (reserve rest for garnish).

2 Combine sesame paste with remaining dressing ingredients and whisk until smooth.

3 Just before serving, toss spinach, cucumber, radish and avocado (if using) together and dress with Japanese Sesame Dressing. Garnish with reserved toasted sesame seeds.

ENERGY	CARBS	PROTEIN	FAT	SAT FAT	SUGARS
376kj / 90kcal	2.6g	2.0g	7.7g	1.6g	2.5g

Peking duck lettuce wraps

SERVES 6 **PREP TIME** 25 minutes **COOK TIME** 10 minutes

DF | GF (use GF soy sauce)

HOISIN SAUCE

oil a drizzle
garlic 1 clove, minced
fresh ginger, finely grated, 2 teaspoons
soy sauce 3 tablespoons
smooth peanut butter (or almond butter) 1½ tablespoons
brown sugar 1½ tablespoons
rice vinegar 1 tablespoon
sesame oil 2 teaspoons
Chinese five spice ½ teaspoon
black pepper ¼ teaspoon
water 2–3 tablespoons

duck breasts 2, at room temperature
Chinese five spice ½ teaspoon
salt to season
spring onions 2–3, green part only
Lebanese cucumber 1 (or ½ telegraph cucumber)
baby cos lettuce leaves 12 (about 2 baby cos lettuces)
roasted peanuts, finely chopped, ¼ cup
red chilli 1, finely chopped or sliced (optional)
lime 1, cut into wedges

I've taken the traditional Peking duck pancakes you find in Chinese restaurants and replaced the pancakes with lettuce leaves and used a home-made hoisin sauce (much easier than you may think, though you can use store-bought if you like). Everyone can make up their own little wraps, so you just have to plonk a platter of the ingredients on the table. Chicken can be used in place of duck if you prefer.

1 Preheat oven to 200°C. Heat oil in a small saucepan on medium heat. Sizzle garlic and ginger for 1 minute, then add remaining Hoisin Sauce ingredients. Whisk to combine and simmer for a few minutes until thickened. Set aside to cool.

2 Pat duck breasts dry with paper towels and trim off any excess overhanging fat. Score the skin, 1cm apart, with a sharp knife. Rub five spice over both sides and season well with salt.

3 Heat a large fry pan on medium heat. Cook breasts, without any oil, skin-side down, for 3–4 minutes until golden brown. Most of the fat will render out of the skin. Flip breasts over and transfer to the oven to cook for 7–8 minutes or until cooked to medium. Remove from oven and set aside to rest for 10 minutes before slicing as thinly as you can.

4 Finely shred or slice spring onion. Place in a bowl of cold water to keep it fresh and crunchy until ready to serve. Cut cucumber into thin batons, discarding the seeds. Separate lettuce leaves and wash gently under cold water to remove any soil.

5 Place cucumber, drained spring onion and lettuce leaves on a platter and serve with a plate of the sliced duck, peanuts, chilli and lime, and a bowl of the Hoisin Sauce on the side. To assemble, place a few slices of duck, some cucumber and spring onion in a lettuce leaf. Drizzle with a little Hoisin Sauce, garnish with peanuts and chilli and squeeze over lime just before eating. You can either assemble to serve ready to eat, or let everyone assemble their own.

ENERGY	CARBS		
1093kj / 261kcal	5.6g		
PROTEIN	**FAT**	**SAT FAT**	**SUGARS**
30.1g	12.9g	2.8g	4.4g

Turmeric pea and spinach rice

SERVES 4–6 **PREP TIME** 5 minutes
COOK TIME 25 minutes   **DF** (omit butter) **I GF**

When you want your Indian meal to be that extra bit special, it's nice to have a rice dish that's a little more interesting than plain rice — but doesn't require more effort to make.

basmati rice 1½ cups
water 2¼ cups
ground turmeric ½ teaspoon
salt a good pinch
butter 15g
frozen peas 2 cups, defrosted
baby spinach 2 handfuls

1 Combine rice, water, turmeric and salt in a medium-sized pot and bring to the boil. As soon as it boils, cover with a tight-fitting lid and reduce to low heat to cook for 15 minutes.

2 After 15 minutes, turn off the heat and leave the rice, still covered, to sit and steam for a further 10–15 minutes before removing the lid.

3 Fluff up turmeric rice with a fork, and toss through butter, peas and spinach.

ENERGY		CARBS	
1215kj / 291kcal		46.9g	
PROTEIN	**FAT**	**SAT FAT**	**SUGARS**
8.4g	6.9g	4.0g	1.0g

Cucumber mint salad

SERVES 4
PREP TIME 5–10 minutes   **DF I GF**

This is a simple, refreshing and cooling side that's a great accompaniment to any curry.

telegraph cucumber 1, cut in half lengthways and sliced
mint leaves, chopped, ¼ cup
lemon zest of ½ and juice of 1
extra-virgin olive oil a drizzle
salt and pepper

1 Toss all ingredients together and season to taste with salt and pepper.

ENERGY		CARBS	
52kj / 12.6kcal		1.9g	
PROTEIN	**FAT**	**SAT FAT**	**SUGARS**
0.7g	0.1g	0g	1.7g

Mexican street corn

*This is the best way I know to eat fresh corn. Don't get me wrong, I love corn on the cob with nothing but butter and salt, but this way just takes it to a whole new level of mouth-watering goodness. It's no wonder this corn dish is sold **everywhere** on the streets of Mexico.*

whole corn cobs 6, husks and silks removed
olive oil
salt
mayonnaise 2 tablespoons
melted butter 1 tablespoon
smoked paprika ¼ teaspoon
cayenne pepper (or chilli powder) ¼ teaspoon
parmesan cheese, finely grated, ¼ cup
limes 2, cut into wedges, to serve

1 Preheat barbecue to medium-high heat (alternatively heat a large, heavy-based fry pan on medium-high heat).

2 Brush corn cobs with oil and season with salt. Grill on the barbecue, or in a pan, until slightly charred all over and kernels are bright yellow, about 10 minutes.

3 Mix mayonnaise with melted butter. Transfer corn to a serving plate and, while the corn is still hot, brush generously with mayonnaise mixture, and sprinkle with smoked paprika, cayenne pepper and parmesan. Serve immediately with lime wedges to squeeze over just before eating.

ENERGY	CARBS	PROTEIN	FAT	SAT FAT	SUGARS
756kj / 181kcal	18.8g	5.7g	8.6g	3.1g	5g

Bombay potatoes

SERVES 4 **PREP TIME** 10 minutes
COOK TIME 25 minutes   **DF | GF**

These Indian-spiced potatoes are ridiculously delicious and moreish. They make a great side to an Indian meal, but sometimes I just serve them with a poached or fried egg for a simple, tasty meal.

Agria potatoes 4 medium (600–700g), scrubbed (leave skin on) and cut into 3cm pieces
oil 2 tablespoons
onion 1 large, diced
mustard seeds 1 teaspoon
curry powder 1 teaspoon
salt ½ teaspoon
baby spinach 2–3 handfuls
red or green chilli 1, finely sliced (optional)

1 Boil potatoes in a pot of well-salted water for about 12 minutes, or until just tender. Drain well, return to the pot and sit over a low heat for a few minutes to steam and 'dry off' the potatoes a little. Shake the pot to 'rough up' the edges of the potatoes.

2 In a wok or your largest fry pan, heat oil and cook onion for 3–4 minutes until soft and starting to turn golden. Add another drizzle of oil, mustard seeds and curry powder, and cook for 1 minute, until fragrant.

3 Add cooked potatoes and salt to the pan and toss to coat in the spiced oil and onions. Keep cooking for 5–8 minutes until potatoes are golden, tossing every now and again. (Try to get a little golden, crunchy crust on some of the potatoes.)

4 Toss spinach through potatoes until wilted, then garnish with fresh chilli (if using).

ENERGY		CARBS	
809kj / 193kcal		25.6g	
PROTEIN	**FAT**	**SAT FAT**	**SUGARS**
4.6g	7.5g	1.2g	0.7g

Coconut green beans

SERVES 4 **PREP TIME** 5 minutes
COOK TIME 5 minutes   **DF | GF**

I got this idea from a favourite Indian restaurant of mine. It's such a simple yet delicious side for any type of Asian meal, and not just Indian, it goes well with South East Asian dishes too.

round green beans 300g, trimmed
desiccated coconut ¼ cup
oil or coconut oil 1 tablespoon
mustard seeds 1 teaspoon
salt

1 Place beans in a large heatproof bowl or a pot. Pour over boiling water to cover and leave for 2–3 minutes to cook lightly. Drain well and pat dry with paper towels.

2 In a large dry (no oil) fry pan, very lightly toast coconut for about 1 minute on medium heat or until a light golden colour. Tip coconut into a bowl and set aside. Leave pan on the heat.

3 Add oil or coconut oil to hot pan and, when it has melted, add mustard seeds and cook for about 30–60 seconds, until they start popping. Add green beans and cook for 1–2 minutes. Take off heat, add toasted coconut, season with salt and toss together.

ENERGY		CARBS	
380kj / 91kcal		2.6g	
PROTEIN	**FAT**	**SAT FAT**	**SUGARS**
1.6g	7.8g	6.3g	1.9g

Juicy garlic 'n herb roast mushrooms

SERVES 4 **PREP TIME** 10 minutes **COOK TIME** 15 minutes   **DF | GF**

balsamic vinegar 2 tablespoons
olive oil 2 tablespoons
liquid honey 1½ teaspoons
brown sugar a pinch
garlic 2 cloves, minced
rosemary or thyme leaves, finely
chopped, 1 tablespoon
portobello mushrooms 10–12 large,
stalks trimmed
salt and pepper, to season
parsley (or chives), finely chopped,
¼ cup, to garnish (optional)

Roasted with a simple balsamic and herb marinade, these mushrooms are the best (if you're a mushroom lover). They make a great side dish or base for a vegetarian meal, or simply serve them with poached eggs for brekkie!

1 Preheat oven to 190°C. Mix balsamic vinegar, olive oil, honey, brown sugar, garlic and rosemary or thyme together.

2 Place mushrooms in a baking dish, gill-side up. Spoon marinade over mushrooms, and season with salt and pepper. Bake for 15 minutes until mushrooms are soft and juicy. Sprinkle with parsley or chives to serve, if you like.

Tip

Don't wash your mushrooms (they soak up too much moisture). Instead, brush off any soil with a pastry brush or paper towel.

	ENERGY	CARBS
	374kj / 89.5kcal	2.3g

PROTEIN	FAT	SAT FAT	SUGARS
4.5g	5.9g	1g	2.1g

Moreish...

Maple and spice-roast carrots

SERVES 4–6   **PREP TIME** 10 minutes   **COOK TIME** 30 minutes   **DF | GF**

baby carrots (or large carrots)
800g–1kg, scrubbed
olive oil 1 tablespoon
maple syrup 1 tablespoon
ground cumin ½ teaspoon
ground coriander ¼ teaspoon
ground turmeric ¼ teaspoon
salt and pepper
flat-leaf parsley or coriander, chopped,
½ cup

I'm not a big fan of boiled carrots, but give me roast carrots any day. Especially these ones: roasted until they're caramelised on the edges, slightly shrivelled and their sweetness intensified, with lovely savoury spices. Great with any roast (especially lamb) and a yoghurt dressing.

1 Preheat oven to 200°C. Line an oven tray with baking paper.

2 If using baby carrots, trim off the tops and tails. If using large carrots, peel and cut into 1cm-thick batons.

3 Toss carrots with olive oil, maple syrup and spices in prepared tray. Season with salt and pepper and roast for 25–30 minutes or until carrots are caramelised and golden.

4 Gently toss with parsley or coriander just before serving.

Tip

You can use 1 teaspoon curry powder in place of spices.

ENERGY	CARBS	PROTEIN	FAT	SAT FAT	SUGARS
343kj / 82kcal	8.7g	1.5g	3.5g	0.6g	8.2g

Gooey baked camembert with plum and beetroot chutney

SERVES 4–5 **PREP TIME** 15 minutes **COOK TIME** 20 minutes

GF (serve with GF bread or crackers)

PLUM, BEETROOT AND RED ONION CHUTNEY

olive oil 2 tablespoons
red onion 1, finely diced
beetroot 1 medium, peeled and finely diced
dried currants ¼ cup (optional)
red wine vinegar ¼ cup
sugar 3½ tablespoons
red-fleshed plums 1 cup diced (use a dark red-fleshed plum, e.g. Omega, or canned plums if not in season)
salt and pepper

BAKED CAMEMBERT

camembert (or brie) 1 large round (about 250g)
rosemary or thyme leaves 1 tablespoon
extra-virgin olive oil a drizzle
freshly ground black pepper

TO SERVE

bread (e.g. ciabatta or sourdough)

Baked camembert (or brie) is the easiest thing to do (you pretty much just slice off the top and bung it in the oven) and it produces a gloriously oozy, melty, gooey, cheesy centrepiece for the table with some toasted bread and chutney. Of course, you can just use a good shop-bought chutney, but here is a lovely fruity plum and beetroot one if you feel like making it yourself. Great as a shared appetizer — although there can be a bit of a fight for it — or served after dinner instead of a cheeseboard.

1 To make the chutney, heat olive oil in a fry pan on medium heat. Cook onion, beetroot and currants (if using) for 10–15 minutes, until soft.

2 Stir in vinegar, sugar and plums. Simmer for about 10 minutes, stirring frequently to avoid burning on the bottom of the pan, until reduced and thickened. Season to taste with salt and pepper (and a little more sugar if needed). The chutney will keep in the fridge for about a week.

3 To bake the cheese, preheat oven to 180°C. Score a 0.5cm border around the top of the camembert, and thinly slice the rind off the top surface, being careful not to remove too much of the cheese inside. Place in a large ramekin or small oven-proof dish so that it fits snugly, cut-side up. Alternatively, place back in its box lined with a bit of baking paper. Sprinkle with herbs, drizzle with extra-virgin olive oil and grind over plenty of black pepper. Bake for 15–20 minutes or until melted and gooey. Halfway through cooking, you can throw some thin slices of bread in the oven on a tray to toast for about 10 minutes.

4 To serve, place baked camembert, a small bowl of chutney and toasted bread on the table and let everyone help themselves.

ENERGY	CARBS		
1610kj / 380kcal	20.4g		

PROTEIN	FAT	SAT FAT	SUGARS
9.3g	29.6g	16.6g	20.2g

Chorizo, tomato, courgette and haloumi skewers

dry-cured chorizo 100–150g
courgettes 1–2 small
haloumi 200g
cherry tomatoes 1 punnet (about 250g)
bamboo wooden skewers
olive oil, for cooking
coriander leaves to garnish

CREAMY CHIPOTLE DIPPING SAUCE
mayonnaise 2 tablespoons
natural unsweetened yoghurt
2 tablespoons
chipotle sauce 2 teaspoons (see Note
page 37)

These tasty little skewers are the ideal nibble to hand around: easy to prepare, quick to cook and popular with everyone. If you're entertaining, you can prepare them the day before, then cook when ready to serve. They can be cooked on the barbecue or in a fry pan.

1 Slice chorizo and courgettes into 1cm-thick rounds. Cut haloumi into 1.5cm cubes and pat dry with paper towels.

2 Thread a piece of chorizo or courgette, then haloumi, then a cherry tomato onto each skewer, going right through the middle of each ingredient so that they all sit more or less flush with each other. This will ensure they make surface contact with the barbecue (or grill pan) during cooking.

3 Brush skewers with oil, if cooking on the barbecue, or heat a drizzle of oil in a grill pan or large fry pan. Cook skewers for 1–2 minutes on each side, or until the chorizo is starting to render out a little fat, the haloumi is golden, and cherry tomatoes are starting to blister. It can help to use a fish slice to flatten them slightly while cooking.

4 Mix mayonnaise, yoghurt and chipotle sauce together.

5 Pile skewers on a plate and garnish with coriander. Serve with a small bowl of Creamy Chipotle Dipping Sauce on the side.

ENERGY	CARBS	PROTEIN	FAT	SAT FAT	SUGARS
662kj / 158kcal	1.6g	8.1g	13.3g	6.2g	1.5g

Chermoula
(for chicken + roast pumpkin and almond salad)

MAKES ¾–1 cup **PREP TIME** 10 minutes   **DF** (without yoghurt) | **GF**

This herby, lemony, garlicky sauce and marinade is super useful as a dressing or dip (by itself or mixed with some yoghurt), a marinade (on meat, fish and vegetables) or as a sauce (on the side to meat, fish, chicken, vegetables or even a stew or curry). As you can see, it is goes with pretty much everything!

coriander leaves and stalks, roughly chopped, 1 cup
parsley, roughly chopped, ¼ cup
garlic 4 cloves, chopped
lemon finely grated zest and juice of 1
white wine vinegar 1 tablespoon
ground cumin 1 tablespoon
ground coriander 1½ teaspoons
smoked paprika 2 teaspoons
red chilli 1 large, chopped
olive oil 3–4 tablespoons
salt ¾ teaspoon

Storage

Store chermoula in the fridge. Will keep for up to 2 weeks or can be frozen for months.

1 Blend all ingredients together in a food processor or blender until well combined. Use in lots of recipes, like the ones below.

Chermoula chicken kebabs

SERVES 4–6

Marinate 600g boneless, skinless **chicken thighs** cut into bite-sized pieces in **chermoula** for an hour or overnight. Thread onto bamboo skewers, season with **salt** then grill or barbecue on high heat.

Chermoula roast pumpkin and almond salad

SERVES 4–6 as a side

Roast 500–600g chunks of **pumpkin** and 2 **red onions** cut into wedges, tossed with a few tablespoons of **chermoula**, a drizzle of **olive oil**, **honey** and **salt** and **pepper**, until soft and slightly caramelised. Toss with ½ cup chopped **roast almonds** and 4 handfuls **salad leaves**. Drizzle with a dressing made of ½ cup **natural unsweetened yoghurt** mixed with a few teaspoons of **chermoula** to taste.

Sticky chilli sauce

MAKES about ¾ cup **PREP TIME** 15 minutes **COOK TIME** 10 minutes   **DF | GF**

oil 1 tablespoon
red capsicum 1, cored and finely diced
garlic 2–3 cloves, minced
ginger, finely chopped or grated,
2 tablespoons
fresh turmeric 3cm piece, finely grated
(or ½ teaspoon ground turmeric),
optional
red chillies 3 large (2 de-seeded and
1 with seeds in — leave the seeds in all
3 for a really hot chilli sauce), finely
chopped
orange juice (freshly squeezed) ⅔ cup
rice vinegar 3 tablespoons
liquid honey 2–3 tablespoons
sugar 2–3 tablespoons
lime juice of 1
salt ¼ teaspoon
water ¼ cup

I find most of the sweet chilli sauces you can buy too sugary and lacking zing. So I decided to make my own, significantly cutting down on the amount of added sugar and with more flavour. The result is one hell of a delicious chilli sauce that goes with just about anything — it's hard to have the bought stuff once you've tried this and experienced how easy it is to make.

1 Heat oil in a fry pan on medium heat. Add capsicum and cook for about 3 minutes or until soft.

2 Add a drizzle more oil, garlic, ginger and turmeric (if using) and continue cooking for a further minute.

3 Add remaining ingredients, bring to a boil and cook for about 10 minutes, stirring often, until thickened. It will continue to thicken and become stickier as it cools.

Storage

Store in the fridge.
Will keep for a couple
of weeks or can
be frozen.

ENERGY	CARBS	PROTEIN	FAT	SAT FAT	SUGARS
287kj / 66kcal	12.3g	0.6g	1.8g	0.1g	11.9g

(per 2 tablespoon serving)

sweet delights with a healthier twist

NOT-TOO-NAUGHTY

BAKING, TREATS AND DESSERTS, HOME-MADE WITH MORE GOODNESS

Jam 'n cream coconut flour sponge sandwich

SERVES 8 **PREP TIME** 15 minutes **COOK TIME** 30 minutes

GF

butter 150g (or 120g coconut oil), softened
caster sugar ¾ cup (or ½ cup honey)
vanilla essence or extract 1½ teaspoons
free-range eggs 4, at room temperature
coconut flour 100g
baking powder 2 teaspoons
milk ⅓ cup

TO ASSEMBLE
Raspberry Chia Jam (page 20) ¾ cup + extra for top of cake
cream 300ml, lightly whipped
fresh berries (e.g. strawberries, raspberries, blackberries)
icing sugar, to dust

Tip
• If you don't have two sponge or cake tins, you can cook all the batter in one round cake tin, for 35–40 minutes, then cut sponge in half horizontally once cool.
• You can also cook sponge in a square tin for 35–40 minutes if using for Baby Coconut Sponge Lamingtons (page 174).

My gluten-intolerant sister was over the moon when I developed this recipe, having been deprived of cream and jam sponge for a few years. Coconut flour soaks up more moisture than other flours (so it's more of a moist sponge cake rather than the super-airy variety) and has a really delicious flavour. You can make it dairy-free, and it's pretty versatile: it's used in my Baby Coconut Sponge Lamingtons on page 174; it eats well warm as a pudding or at room temperature filled with cream and fruit, and is awesome in a trifle.

1 Preheat oven to 180°C. Lightly grease and line the base and sides of two 18-20cm cake or sponge tins with baking paper.

2 In a large mixing bowl, beat butter, sugar and vanilla until pale, thick and fluffy. Use an electric beater, or a wooden spoon and plenty of elbow grease! (Note: if you're using coconut oil and honey, it won't fluff up or change much, but don't worry, it's what to expect.)

3 Beat in eggs, one at a time, making sure each egg is fully incorporated after each addition. Continue beating until light and fluffy.

4 In another bowl, sift coconut flour and baking powder together. Add to creamed mixture, along with milk, and fold together with a large metal spoon until batter is well combined — it will be very thick and hold its shape.

5 Spoon into prepared cake tins, smooth out the top and bake for about 30 minutes until light golden on top and cakes spring back when gently pressed in the middle. Leave to cool in the tin for about 10 minutes before turning out. Once cool, sandwich cakes with Raspberry Chia Jam and whipped cream. Top with more Raspberry Chia Jam, fresh berries and a dusting of icing sugar.

ENERGY	CARBS	PROTEIN	FAT	SAT FAT	SUGARS
1820kj / 429kcal	28g	7.0g	32.5g	19.8g	25.2g

Persian love cake with labne icing

SERVES 8 **PREP TIME** 15 minutes **COOK TIME** 45 minutes   **DF** (use coconut oil + coconut yoghurt) | **GF**

This beautiful, fragrant and festive-looking cake apparently gets its name from a love story of a woman who made a cake for a Persian prince to get him to fall in love with her. If true, I'm sure she succeeded, as it's a pretty charming cake! If making the labne (which is just strained yoghurt) icing, allow 6–8 hours of fridge time. It makes a fantastic 'icing' with its thick, spreadable consistency and perfect tang to balance out the cake's sweetness. For something simpler, just serve the cake (un-iced) with a dollop of yoghurt on the side.

LABNE ICING
natural Greek yoghurt 1 cup

CAKE
butter 125g, softened (or 100g coconut oil)
honey (or brown sugar) ¾ cup
orange zest of 1
lemon zest of 1
vanilla essence or extract 1 teaspoon
free-range eggs 4, at room temperature
natural Greek yoghurt ½ cup
ground almonds 2½ cups
salt a good pinch
baking soda 1 level teaspoon

TO GARNISH
pomegranate seeds of ½
pistachios ⅓ cup, shelled and chopped
orange zest of 1

1 To make Labne Icing, line a sieve with muslin cloth or a paper towel and sit it over a bowl with high sides. Place yoghurt in the lined sieve. Cover with clingfilm and refrigerate for 6–8 hours (or overnight) to allow liquid to drain off the yoghurt, resulting in a very thick yoghurt cheese, much the same consistency as mascarpone or whipped cream cheese.

2 Preheat oven to 180°C. Lightly grease and line the base and sides of a 20–21cm round cake tin with baking paper.

3 If you have a food processor, blitz all cake ingredients together until smooth. If you don't have a food processor, beat butter, honey, zests and vanilla together in a large mixing bowl until pale.

4 Beat in eggs, one at a time, making sure each egg is fully incorporated before adding the next one. Mix in yoghurt, ground almonds, salt and baking soda until well combined.

5 Spoon into prepared cake tin. Bake for about 45 minutes or until the top is deep golden and a skewer inserted into the centre comes out pretty much clean. Allow cake to cool to room temperature before icing.

6 To serve, spread Labne Icing over cake and decorate with pomegranate seeds, pistachios, orange zest, and a drizzle more of honey if desired.

Tips

• If you don't have time to make the Labne Icing, use cream cheese beaten with a little lemon juice to make it a bit tart, like yoghurt.
• Soak shelled pistachios in cold water for 30–60 minutes to slightly soften and make it easy to rub off skins revealing bright green underneath.

ENERGY	CARBS	PROTEIN	FAT	SAT FAT	SUGARS
2114kj / 505kcal	36.2g	13g	35.8g	12.1g	29.2g

Watermelon 'cake'

SERVES 8–10   **PREP TIME** 20 minutes + about 3 hours chill time in the fridge   **GF**

When Bodhi turned one, I wanted a cake for him to have a candle in so we could mark the occasion and all sing happy birthday (and get a good photo!). However, at that age, you don't really want to start them on sugar- and white flour-laden treats when they don't really care. His favourite food on earth is watermelon, so I made him this watermelon 'cake' which was an absolute hit with him and his little friends (and the adults!). It's so simple to make, the key is just getting a good, as large as you can find, watermelon.

watermelon 1 large
cream cheese 250g, softened
lemon finely grated zest of ½
vanilla essence 1 teaspoon
maple syrup 1–2 tablespoons
cream 1 cup
fresh fruit (e.g. fresh berries, orange, kiwifruit, passionfruit) to decorate

1 Slice the top and bottom off watermelon so that the top and bottom are flat. Cut skin off watermelon, then go around with the knife once again to tidy it up and get a more or less cylindrical shape (it doesn't have to be perfectly cylindrical though, avoid cutting off too much watermelon). Store in the fridge for a couple of hours until nice and cold (this helps the icing stick to it better).

2 To make the icing, use an electric beater on high speed to beat cream cheese, zest, vanilla and maple syrup together in a large bowl. Beat until smooth and there are no lumps. Add cream and continue beating on low to medium speed until a thick, spreadable consistency, about 2–3 minutes. Once it is thickened, only beat on low speed to avoid overbeating.

3 Place icing in fridge for at least 3 hours to firm up (this will make it easier when it comes to icing time). You can keep the icing in the fridge, well covered (so it doesn't take on any 'fridge flavours') for up to a couple of days until ready to use.

4 When ready to ice the 'cake', place watermelon on a serving plate or cake stand and thoroughly pat dry with paper towels. Spoon cold icing onto watermelon and gently spread over the top and sides with a palette or butter knife. You can keep the iced 'cake' in the fridge for several hours until ready to serve. If any of the icing has slipped off don't worry (this has happened more than once to me!), just spread it back up the sides and it will stick. Decorate with fresh fruit, a candle and your child's favourite little toy and serve!

ENERGY	CARBS	PROTEIN	FAT	SAT FAT	SUGARS
1418kj / 339kcal	30g	3.3g	22.5g	13.3g	30g

Carrot 'n cranberry date loaf

MAKES 1 loaf, enough for 8 slices/servings
PREP TIME 10 minutes **COOK TIME** 1 hour

DF (use coconut oil) **| GF** (use a mix of buckwheat and GF flour)

dried dates 1 cup
water ½ cup
baking soda 1½ level teaspoons
butter or coconut oil 50g
maple syrup (or liquid honey)
⅓ cup
vanilla essence or extract 1 teaspoon
banana (very ripe) 1 large, mashed
grated carrot 2 loosely packed cups
(about 2 carrots)
free-range egg 1, lightly beaten
dried cranberries ¾ cup, chopped
flour (plain, wholemeal, spelt or a
mixture of buckwheat and GF flours)
1½ cups
mixed spice 1 teaspoon

The carrots in this loaf keep it wonderfully moist, and the sweet 'n' sour cranberries give it a tart juicy sweetness that's not too sickly. It makes a great lunchbox filler or morning/ afternoon tea snack.

1 Preheat oven to 170°C. Line a standard size (5–6 cup capacity) loaf tin with baking paper. Place dates and water in a medium-sized pot and boil for about 5 minutes, stirring frequently, until the dates are all mushed up and the water has evaporated. Add baking soda and mix well — it will froth up a little.

2 Mix in butter or coconut oil, maple syrup and vanilla until butter has melted. Then mix in banana, carrot, egg and cranberries until well combined.

3 Sift flour and mixed spice into the pot, and fold the two mixtures together using a large metal spoon until just combined, being careful not to over-mix — a few lumps is fine!

4 Spoon batter into lined loaf tin and roughly smooth out the top. Bake for 1 hour or until a skewer inserted into the centre of the loaf comes out clean. Leave in the tin for 10 minutes before turning out. Best served warm from the oven, or re-warmed briefly in the microwave or oven if eating later.

Storage

Will stay fresh for a few days or freeze slices in an airtight container or resealable bag for a month.

ENERGY	CARBS	PROTEIN	FAT	SAT FAT	SUGARS
1245kj / 297kcal	53g	4.6g	6.5g	3.5g	35.9g

No-sugar banana bread

MAKES 2 small loaves, 12–14 slices   **PREP TIME** 10 minutes
COOK TIME 45 minutes

DF (use coconut oil) | GF (use GF flour)

If Carlos and Bodhi don't get to the bananas before they turn perfectly over-ripe, I'll make this very useful banana bread. It doesn't have any added sugar — with three bananas, (make sure they're very ripe, the spottier the better!) it's naturally sweet enough. It's excellent toasted (which seems to make it even sweeter) and spread with butter, nut-butter, or even creamy ricotta and, if you like, a tiny drizzle of honey.

butter or coconut oil 125g, melted
bananas (very ripe) 3 large, well mashed
desiccated coconut 1½ cups
ground almonds 1 cup
flour (plain, wholemeal, spelt or GF flour) ½ cup
baking soda 1 level teaspoon
vanilla essence or extract 2 teaspoons
salt a pinch
free-range eggs 3, whisked
banana 1, to garnish (optional)
ground cinnamon pinch of, to garnish (optional)

1 Preheat oven to 180°C. Line two small loaf tins (e.g. 3.5 cup capacity) with baking paper.

2 In a large bowl, mix melted butter or coconut oil, mashed banana, coconut, ground almonds, flour, baking soda, vanilla, salt and eggs. Stir until well combined.

3 Spoon mixture into prepared loaf tins, dividing equally. Peel and cut remaining banana (if using) in half lengthways and arrange a banana half on top of each loaf. Sprinkle with cinnamon (if using).

4 Bake for 35–40 minutes or until loaves are golden and a skewer inserted into the centre comes out clean.

5 Leave loaves to cool in tins for 5–10 minutes before removing from tins and transferring to a wire rack. Very yummy toasted and spread with butter!

Storage

Keep in an airtight container for up to 3 days, or in the fridge for up to 5 days. Can also be frozen in an airtight container or resealable bag for a month.

ENERGY	CARBS	PROTEIN	FAT	SAT FAT	SUGARS
1057kj / 249kcal	13g	4.7g	20.1g	12g	7.8g

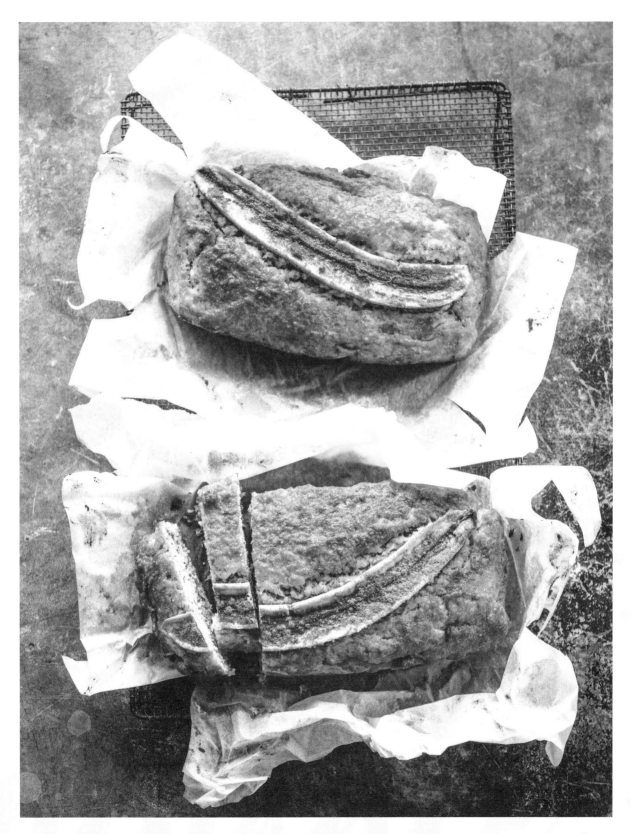

Plum and white chocolate short cake

MAKES 16–20 pieces **PREP TIME** 15 minutes **COOK TIME** 35–40 minutes   **GF** (use mix of buckwheat + GF flour)

butter 150g, softened
sugar (white, brown, rapadura or coconut) ⅓ cup
vanilla essence or extract 1 teaspoon
free-range egg 1, at room temperature
flour 1 cup (e.g. plain, wholemeal, spelt, or a mix of buckwheat and GF flours)
desiccated coconut ½ cup
ground almonds ½ cup
ground cinnamon ½ teaspoon
baking powder 2 teaspoons
salt a pinch
dark-fleshed plums stones removed and chopped, 2 cups (about 8–10 small), (or raspberries, fresh or defrosted and well drained)
white chocolate 100–125g, chopped
almonds (chopped, flaked or slivered) ¼ cup (optional)
icing sugar, to dust (optional)

Crammed with plums and white chocolate, this slice is scrumptious served by itself, or it makes a mighty fine pudding when warmed and served with custard or ice-cream. I've used a blend of flour, coconut and almonds to give more texture and nutty flavour, however, you can just replace the coconut and almonds with more flour (using the same quantities) if you like. Raspberries instead of plums also works magic.

1 Preheat oven to 180°C. Line a 20–22cm square baking tin with baking paper.

2 In a large mixing bowl, beat butter, sugar and vanilla together until light, fluffy and pale (either with an electric beater or a wooden spoon and lots of elbow grease).

3 Beat in egg until well incorporated.

4 Stir in flour, coconut, ground almonds, cinnamon, baking powder and salt until just combined.

5 Spoon two-thirds of batter into lined tin and spread roughly over the base (a wet spoon will help it spread more easily).

6 Scatter with plums and white chocolate, then dot with remaining batter in lumps, and scatter almonds over the top (if using). Press down very gently with the back of a wet spoon. Bake for 35–40 minutes, until golden brown.

7 Leave to cool in the tin for at least 15 minutes before removing and slicing. Dust with a little icing sugar just before serving. Serve at room temperature as a slice or warmed, with custard, as a pudding.

ENERGY	CARBS
831kj / 198kcal	16.1g

PROTEIN	FAT	SAT FAT	SUGARS
3.1g	13.7g	7.5g	10.7g

Baby coconut sponge lamingtons

MAKES 16 small lamingtons **PREP TIME** 40 minutes **COOK TIME** 40 minutes   **GF**

Coconut Flour Sponge Cake (page 160)
cooked in a 20cm square tin instead of a
round tin

CHOCOLATE LAMINGTONS
desiccated coconut 100g
cream 150ml
dark chocolate 125g, chopped

**WHITE CHOCOLATE RASPBERRY
LAMINGTONS**
desiccated coconut 100g
freeze-dried raspberry powder (I used
the brand Fresh-As, available from
gourmet food stores)
1 tablespoon
cream 75ml
white chocolate 150g, chopped

TO SERVE
whipped cream
Raspberry Chia Jam (page 20, or
shop-bought raspberry jam)

*When I was a kid I could never go past a lamington from
the bakery, but now I find them on the dry side (not to
mention stingy with the whipped cream and jam!). Say
hello to these babies! I've used my (gluten-free) coconut
flour sponge, coated in real chocolate and coconut, then
crammed with whipped cream and my super-fruity
Raspberry Chia Jam. They're moist, light and delicious
— and will delight anyone lucky enough to gobble one!*

1 Bake Coconut Flour Sponge Cake (in a 20cm square tin
instead of a round tin) using recipe on page 160. Once
removed from the tin, store in the fridge, uncovered, for
1–2 hours to firm up (it firms the sponge up slightly,
making it less crumbly and easier to cut). When ready to
make lamingtons, trim edges off sponge cake, then cut
into 16 neat squares.

2 For Chocolate Lamingtons, place coconut in a bowl.
Gently heat cream in microwave or on stovetop, then stir
in the chocolate until melted and a smooth, silky ganache
forms. Leave to cool. Once cooled, dip in each piece of
sponge and spread with chocolate over all sides (using a
butter knife), then roll generously in coconut.

continued over page...

3 For White Chocolate Raspberry Lamingtons, mix coconut with freeze-dried raspberry powder in a bowl. Gently heat cream in microwave or on stovetop, then stir in the white chocolate until melted and a smooth, silky ganache forms. Leave to cool. Once cooled, dip each piece of sponge and spread with chocolate over all sides (using a butter knife), then roll generously in raspberry coconut.

4 Place lamingtons in the fridge for about 10 minutes to allow the coating to set, then cut in half, fill with whipped cream and a little dollop of jam.

Tips

• Coating the lamingtons with chocolate can get a little messy. To avoid a sticky mess, use one hand to hold the sponge while dipping and spreading with chocolate, and the other hand for holding the knife and rolling in the coconut.
• If you can't get hold of freeze-dried raspberry powder, just coat the lamingtons in white chocolate and coconut and garnish with a raspberry dipped in a little chocolate (so that it sticks).
• If you are in a hurry and still want lamingtons, and don't care if they're not gluten-free, you could use a good shop-bought sponge and follow the recipe as is.

	ENERGY	CARBS	PROTEIN	FAT	SAT FAT	SUGARS
Chocolate	572kj / 136kcal	5g	1.5g	12.1g	8.3g	4.1g
Raspberry	532kj / 127kcal	7.9g	1.6g	9.9g	6.9g	7.6g

Very fruity crumble slice

MAKES 16 pieces **PREP TIME** 20 minutes **COOK TIME** 35–40 minutes   **DF** (use coconut oil)

This is one of those versatile baking recipes that you can make on a whim, because you're likely to have everything in the pantry and some kind of seasonal fruit in the fruit bowl. Use apricots, plums, nectarines or berries in summer and feijoas or pears in autumn. Delish by itself, but also warmed up and served as pudding.

FILLING
apples (use a variety that holds its shape when cooked e.g. Golden Delicious, Braeburn or Granny Smith) 500g, peeled and chopped
apricot or feijoa flesh 400g, sliced
honey (or sugar) 3 tablespoons
vanilla essence or extract 1 teaspoon
water 2–3 tablespoons

BASE AND CRUMBLE TOPPING
fine (quick cook) rolled oats 2 cups
desiccated coconut 1 cup
medjool dates 12, pitted (or 18–20 dried dates soaked in hot water for 5 minutes until soft, then well drained)
vanilla essence or extract 1 teaspoon
salt a good pinch
mixed spice 1 teaspoon
ground cinnamon 1 teaspoon
butter or coconut oil, melted, ½ cup
honey 2 teaspoons

1 Preheat oven to 180°C. Line a 20cm square baking tin with baking paper.

2 Place apples and half of the apricot or feijoa flesh (reserve the other half) in a medium-sized pot with honey, vanilla and water on medium heat. Cover partially and cook, stirring frequently, for 12–15 minutes or until fruit is soft and there is hardly any liquid. Transfer to a bowl and leave to cool in the fridge while you make the base and topping.

3 Blitz all base and crumble topping ingredients in a food processor (or see Tip) until well combined and mixture sticks together when pinched between your fingers. If it seems too dry, add a little more coconut oil or melted butter.

4 Set 1 cup of mixture aside, then press the rest into the base of the prepared tin, using the back of a spoon. Bake for about 15 minutes or until light golden.

5 Spread stewed fruit over the cooked base and top with reserved apricots or feijoas. Scatter with the reserved 1 cup of crumble mixture. Bake for 20–30 minutes or until crumble is golden.

6 Serve at room temperature or cold by itself, or with yoghurt, or warmed with custard or ice-cream for pudding.

Tip

if you don't have a food processor, cook dates with a splash of water in a pot, stirring frequently, until they have broken up and formed a mushy paste. Then mix with remaining base and crumble topping ingredients.

Storage

Will keep in the fridge for up to five days. Can also be frozen in an airtight container.

ENERGY	CARBS	PROTEIN	FAT	SAT FAT	SUGARS
903kj / 216kcal	22.7g	2.6g	11.9g	9.5g	15.6g

SWEET THOUGHTS

We know that too much sugar isn't great for us, but there's no harm in having a little. I reckon the world would be a pretty glum place if we couldn't enjoy something sweet every now and again!

The recipes in this section are comparatively lower in sugar and/or white flour compared with their typical counterparts. I still use sugar in my baking, treats and desserts, but in many cases I will reduce the total amount and replace it with fruit (which still contains natural sugars, but comparatively less, plus the added bonus of vitamins, minerals and fibre). The recipes are more focused on flavours coming from spices, citrus zest, vanilla, nut butter, and different types of flours, rather than having to rely on overwhelming sweetness.

Rest assured, I would never compromise on flavour in favour of something 'healthier' — for a lot of recipes it works to make them that bit healthier, but for others there's just no point. Sometimes you're best just to have the full-sugar, white flour version very occasionally and make sure you really enjoy it! I like to say, aim to eat well 90 percent of the time, but feel free to have whatever you want the other 10 percent of the time.

And that's why I have added a separate section with my top-ten sweet treats for special occasions (pages 216–245) to the 100+ recipes in this book.

For many of these recipes I have given the option of using plain sugar or more naturally occurring sweeteners, such as honey or maple syrup. While these are less refined than white sugar, don't forget that sugar is still sugar (no matter what form it comes in), so my preference when cooking sweet recipes is always to reduce the total amount rather than do a simple swap.

Many of these recipes also use a smaller quantity of white flour than usual. Again, having some is fine, but it has next to no nutrition or fibre. So I will often use a mix of wholemeal flour, or an alternative flour such as buckwheat, spelt or coconut flour, and maybe desiccated coconut or ground almonds. Many recipes also use nut butter (high in healthy, mono-unsaturated fats) or coconut oil as an alternative to butter. As long as the flavour is still fantastic, I'm all for it! As a result, many of these recipes have ended up being dairy and/or gluten-free — it's nice to have options that can be enjoyed by everyone!

Banana 'n blueberry bran muffins

MAKES 12 large muffins **PREP TIME** 10 minutes **COOK TIME** 20–25 minutes | **DF** (use coconut yoghurt)

These might not be the most beautiful muffins you've ever seen, but I'm sure they'll become one of your trusty muffins to make, time and time again (I've probably made them about a hundred times!). Even though they've got a decent amount of bran in them, they're moist, light and sweet thanks to lots of banana and blueberries.

self-raising flour 1 cup
ground cinnamon 2 teaspoons
salt a good pinch
bran flakes (or wheat bran) 1½ cups
sultanas (or raisins) ½ cup (optional)
golden syrup ⅓ cup
oil (e.g. grapeseed) ¼ cup
bananas (very ripe) 3 large, mashed
vanilla essence or extract 1 teaspoon
free-range eggs 2
yoghurt (dairy or coconut) ¾ cup
baking soda (lump-free or sifted)
1 level teaspoon
blueberries (fresh or defrosted and well drained) 1 cup

1 Preheat oven to 200°C. Line a 12-hole muffin tin with paper cases.

2 Sift flour and cinnamon into a medium-sized mixing bowl. Stir in salt, bran flakes and sultanas (if using).

3 In a large mixing bowl, whisk golden syrup, oil, banana, vanilla, eggs, yoghurt and baking soda together until smooth.

4 Add flour mixture to the wet mixture. Fold together with a large metal spoon until just combined — do not over-mix, it's fine if it's a little lumpy (this generally gives lighter muffins). Quickly fold through blueberries.

5 Spoon mixture into paper cases, dividing equally. Bake for 20–25 minutes or until muffins have risen and the tops are light golden and spring back when lightly pressed. Remove from oven and leave to stand for 5 minutes before removing to a wire rack to cool.

Storage

Keep in an airtight container for a few days, or freeze for up to a month.

Tip

For even more fibre, you can substitute self-raising flour with 1 cup wholemeal flour + 1½ teaspoons baking powder.

ENERGY	CARBS	PROTEIN	FAT	SAT FAT	SUGARS
906kj / 216kcal	30.9g	4.7g	7.2g	1.1g	21.2g

183

Lemon and blackberry friands

MAKES 12 **PREP TIME** 15 minutes **COOK TIME** 15–20 minutes   **GF** (use GF flour)

free-range egg whites 2 medium
flour (plain or GF) 2 tablespoons
icing sugar ½ cup
ground almonds ⅓ cup
lemon finely grated zest of 1
butter 60g, melted
blackberries or raspberries 12–24,
fresh or frozen (do not defrost)
icing sugar, to dust

These light, pillowy little mouthfuls are the perfect morsel for eating daintily with a cup of tea.

1 Preheat oven to 180°C. Grease a 12-hole mini muffin tin lightly with butter, then dust with flour. Tip tin to the side and upside down and tap to remove any excess flour (this will help prevent the friands from sticking to the tin, making them easier to remove once cooked).

2 Lightly whisk egg whites in a clean, dry, medium-sized bowl until frothy.

3 Sift flour and icing sugar into the bowl then, using a large metal spoon, fold in ground almonds, lemon zest and melted butter until just combined. Be careful not to overmix as you don't want to knock out any air.

4 Spoon heaped tablespoonsful of mixture into each muffin tin, filling about half full. Top each with a berry or two.

5 Bake for 16–18 minutes, until light golden around the edges. Let them cool in the tin for a few minutes before removing and transferring to a wire rack. You may need to use a knife to help carefully remove friands from the tin. Dust with icing sugar just before serving.

ENERGY	CARBS	PROTEIN	FAT	SAT FAT	SUGARS
364kj / 87kcal	6.9g	1.7g	6.1g	3.1 g	6.3g

Choccy-chip nut butter cookies

MAKES 18–20 cookies **PREP TIME** 10 minutes
COOK TIME 10–15 minutes

DF (check chocolate used) | **GF** (use desiccated coconut)

smooth peanut butter (or almond
butter) ½ cup
fine rolled oats or desiccated coconut
½ cup
brown sugar ½ cup
free-range egg 1 large
vanilla essence or extract ½ teaspoon
chocolate chips (or chopped milk or
dark chocolate, or sultanas) ⅓ cup

Ridiculously quick and easy to make, these cookies make great lunchbox treats or to serve guests when you're short on time. This recipe, using oats or desiccated coconut, results in a softer, flatter and chewier cookie. However, for a denser, richer cookie (like the small ones in the photograph) you can just use 1 cup of nut butter and no oats or coconut.

1 Preheat oven to 180°C. Line a baking tray with baking paper.

2 Mix all ingredients together until well combined.

3 Roll tablespoonsful of mixture and place on prepared baking tray. Flatten slightly with the back of a fork or spoon. Bake for 12–14 minutes or until golden.

4 Remove from oven and allow to cool. If storing, allow to cool completely before placing in an airtight container. Have a couple with a glass of milk — yummo!

ENERGY	CARBS	PROTEIN	FAT	SAT FAT	SUGARS
348kj / 83kcal	7g	2.6g	4.8g	1.6g	5g

Rustic spiced apple pie

SERVES 6–8 **PREP TIME** 10 minutes **COOK TIME** 45 minutes

Braeburn apples (or Granny Smiths)
5 small or 3–4 large, cored
lemon juice 2 tablespoons
mixed spice ¾ teaspoon
ground cinnamon ½ teaspoon
brown sugar 3 tablespoons
sweet shortcrust pastry 350g,
keep cold
ground almonds (or almond meal)
⅓ cup

TO SERVE
icing sugar 2 teaspoons, to dust
**vanilla ice-cream, yoghurt, custard
   or cream**

• Make sure the pastry is kept cold,
as it will be much easier to work with
that way. However, if the pastry does
tear a little don't fret, as shortcrust
pastry is very forgiving — all you
have to do is push/squish it back
together with your fingers, much like
play dough, and it will cook just fine!
• To make this extra indulgent,
drizzle the pie with Salted Caramel
Sauce (page 228).

*This is often plonked on the table after a Sunday night
roast when we have family or friends around. It's the
ideal, minimal-effort, no-fuss dessert that pleases and
comforts when drizzled with custard or cream, or served
with a scoop of ice-cream plopped on top.*

1 Line a baking tray with baking paper.

2 Roughly peel apples (i.e. you can leave some skin on them
— it's nice for a bit of colour and also helps them hold their
shape) and cut into 1–2cm-thick slices. Place apples in a
bowl with lemon juice, mixed spice, cinnamon and half of
the brown sugar, and toss together.

3 Roll out pastry on a lightly floured surface into a rough
30cm diameter circle, about 3mm thick, and place on lined
baking tray.

4 Sprinkle ground almonds over pastry (they help soak up
any juices from the apple), leaving a rough 5cm border
around the edge.

5 Pile apples on top of the ground almonds, then fold the
sides of the pastry up to partially enclose the apples. Pat
and shape the bottom of the pie with your hands to hold it
firmly in place. Sprinkle remaining brown sugar on top.
Place pie in the fridge for 10–15 minutes to allow the pastry
to firm up a little.

6 In the meantime, preheat oven to 180°C. Brush pastry
with egg wash (optional). Bake for about 45 minutes or until
golden brown. Allow to stand for at least 15 minutes before
cutting and serving.

7 Dust with icing sugar and serve warm with yoghurt,
custard, cream or ice-cream.

ENERGY	CARBS
1391kj / 332kcal	39g

PROTEIN	FAT	SAT FAT	SUGARS
4.6g	17.5g	7.6g	14.9g

Creamy coconut rice pudding with spiced pineapple

SERVES 4 **PREP TIME** 15 minutes **COOK TIME** 10 minutes   **DF** (use DF milk + coconut oil) **| GF**

I'm a huge rice pudding fan — it ticks so many boxes: creamy, warm, nourishing and comforting, and I just love the fact that it's cheap to make and the perfect way to use up leftover rice — and leftover canned coconut cream or milk. And, as this is cooked on the stovetop, it's much quicker than the baked version. It's just as yummy with canned fruit for a quick dessert, but if you wanted to make it special enough for guests, make this simple but divine spiced pineapple to go with it.

1 To make the rice pudding, stir everything, except sweetener, together in a pot and simmer on medium heat, stirring frequently (to avoid it burning on the bottom), for 6–8 minutes or until thick and creamy. Stir through sweetener to taste.

2 To make the Spiced Pineapple, heat butter or coconut oil in a large fry pan on medium heat. Add pineapple and spices. Cook for about 5 minutes or until pineapple is soft. Toss with brown sugar and continue cooking for a further 2 minutes or so.

3 To serve, spoon rice pudding into bowls and top with spiced pineapple.

RICE PUDDING
cooked rice (e.g. Jasmine, short grain or long grain, but not basmati) 3 cups (from 1 cup uncooked rice)
coconut milk 1½ cups
milk (of any kind) 1¼ cups
vanilla essence or extract 2 teaspoons
salt a good pinch
sugar (or honey or maple syrup) 2–3 tablespoons

SPICED PINEAPPLE
butter or coconut oil 1 tablespoon
fresh pineapple ½, skin cut off and cored, cut into 2cm cubes
ground cinnamon 1 teaspoon
whole spices (e.g. star anise, cardamom, cloves), lightly bruised
brown sugar 1 tablespoon

Tip

Add a few slices of fresh ginger or a torn kaffir lime leaf to the rice pudding for a subtle aromatic flavour.

ENERGY	CARBS	PROTEIN	FAT	SAT FAT	SUGARS
1792kj / 428kcal	52.8g	6.2g	20.5g	15.8g	28.1g

Arabian fruit salad (and a really cool ice bowl)

SERVES 6 **PREP TIME** 40 minutes + overnight to freeze ice bowl   **DF | GF**

An ice bowl is a guaranteed way to get lots of ooohs and ahhhhs at dessert time. They're surprisingly easy to make: use whatever herbs, citrus, flowers and berries you like — get creative! Once the ice bowl has frozen hard, it will not only look magnificent, but do a great job of keeping the contents chilled too. This fragrant rosewater-scented fruit salad tastes as exotic as it looks, with its little ruby jewels but, seriously, anything will look beautiful in the ice bowl!

1 To make the ice bowl, start by placing orange and lime slices, rose buds and petals on the inside of the large bowl — it helps to stack the citrus slices on top of each other, and wedge roses, leaves and petals in between to help them stay in place.

2 Place smaller bowl inside and continue to position and place citrus and roses in the gap between the two bowls — a wooden skewer or chopstick to help poke them down may be helpful.

3 Fill the smaller bowl with ice cubes and/or water to help weigh it down. Then slowly pour cold water (using a jug) between the bowls to 0.5–1cm from the top. Carefully transfer to a flat surface in the freezer and freeze overnight (or longer) until frozen solid.

continued over page...

ICE BOWL
What you will need:
bowls 2, one large, and one smaller
(that can fit inside the larger one, with a
1.5–2.5cm gap between them)
oranges 2, sliced 1–1.5cm thick
limes 3–4, sliced 1–1.5cm thick
rose buds, flowers, petals and leaves
a jug
cold water
ice cubes a few handfuls
...and space in your freezer to fit the bowl!

FRUIT SALAD
rose water 3 tablespoons (see Tip,
page 196)
lemon juice or lime juice freshly
squeezed, ¼ cup
orange juice of 1
sugar (or liquid honey) 2 teaspoons
mint leaves, finely chopped,
3 tablespoons
watermelon ½, skin removed and diced
honeydew melon 1 small or ½ large, skin
removed and diced
oranges 4, skin removed and diced
pomegranate seeds of ½

4 When ready to use, take out of freezer and stand on the bench for about 10 minutes to thaw slightly or until the inside bowl lifts away easily. Carefully turn the large bowl upside-down on a tea towel to remove ice bowl — it may take a few minutes to fall out, so be patient! Return ice bowl to the freezer until ready to serve (you can freeze it for weeks).

5 To make the fruit salad, mix rose water, lemon or lime juice, orange juice, sugar and mint until sugar is dissolved, then toss with fruit. Spoon into ice bowl to serve. Place a cloth or tea towel underneath to catch any drips as it slowly melts (but don't worry, it will last for the duration of your dessert!)

Tips

• The ice bowl will keep for weeks in your freezer and can be reused a few times. It's a great serving vessel for scoops of ice-cream too!
• You can buy rosewater from gourmet food stores (or the international section of some supermarkets). But you can leave it out if you prefer.

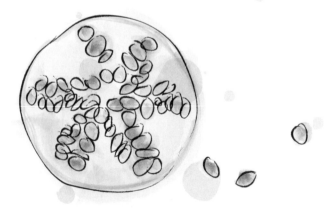

ENERGY	CARBS	PROTEIN	FAT	SAT FAT	SUGARS
1928kj / 461kcal	94.7g	9.6g	2.9g	0.1g	93.2g

Nutty bananary chocolate fudge

MAKES 16–20 pieces **PREP TIME** 10 minutes + at least 1 hour in the freezer

DF | GF

smooth nut butter (e.g. cashew nut, almond, hazelnut, peanut or a blend) ½ cup

coconut oil 3 tablespoons

maple syrup 3 tablespoons

dark cocoa powder (I like to use Dutch cocoa powder) 2 tablespoons

banana (ripe) 1, well mashed (until there are no lumps — do it on a chopping board)

salt a good pinch

vanilla essence or extract 1 teaspoon

lemon juice or balsamic vinegar 1 teaspoon

coconut chips, pistachios and freeze-dried fruit to garnish (optional)

Who ever thought that you could make a healthy chocolate fudge that was sweet, buttery, soft and fudgy enough to be worth eating? With the help of banana and nut butter, this has the same soft fudgy, slightly gooey texture that you want in any good fudge and is healthy enough that even one-year-old Bodhi is allowed a piece.

1 Combine nut butter, coconut oil and maple syrup in a medium saucepan and gently heat to melt the coconut oil. Stir everything together until smooth.

2 Mix in cocoa, mashed banana, salt, vanilla and lemon juice or balsamic vinegar until smooth.

3 Spoon mixture into a small dish (I use a rectangle 11–15cm one) or loaf tin lined with baking paper and spread to the sides. Sprinkle over nuts, coconut and freeze-dried fruit (if using). Freeze for at least 1 hour until firm.

4 Remove by lifting out baking paper, then cut into 16–20 pieces. Store covered in the freezer.

Storage

Store in an airtight container in the freezer. Will keep for 3–4 weeks.

ENERGY	CARBS	PROTEIN	FAT	SAT FAT	SUGARS
302kj / 72kcal	4.2g	1.9g	5.2g	2.5g	3.7g

Munchy muesli bars

MAKES 12 bars **PREP TIME** 15 minutes
COOK TIME 20 minutes + 3 hours in the fridge

DF (use coconut oil + check chocolate)
GF (use quinoa flakes)

smooth peanut butter (or almond butter) ½ cup (or see Tip to make nut-free)
liquid honey 2 tablespoons
coconut oil or butter, melted, 1½ tablespoons
rolled oats (or quinoa flakes) ½ cup
chia seeds 2 tablespoons
sunflower seeds ¼ cup
shredded or thread coconut ½ cup
dried fruit (e.g. dried cherries, cranberries, apricots or dates), chopped, ½ cup
pumpkin seeds ¼ cup
salt a pinch
dark chocolate chips (or chopped dark chocolate) ½ cup

Tip

To make these nut-free, take out the nut butter and replace with ½ cup chopped dried dates. Boil dates in a pot with ⅓ cup water, stirring frequently, until a mushy paste forms — this will help hold the ingredients together.

Storage

Store in an airtight container in the fridge (they'll keep for 1–2 weeks). Or freeze in an airtight container or resealable bag for 1–2 months.

So quick to throw together, you will end up making these regularly for lunchboxes or those mornings when you have to do a grab-and-run breakfast. They're significantly lower in sugar than bought muesli bars and, of course, have no weird e-numbers. If you like, you can cut them into smaller squares to make cute muesli 'bites' for little treats. They also freeze well, so you can make a couple of batches.

1 Preheat oven to 150°C. Line a 20cm square baking tin with baking paper.

2 Stir nut butter, honey and coconut oil or butter together until smooth.

3 Add oats, chia seeds, sunflower seeds, coconut, dried fruit, pumpkin seeds and salt and stir together until well combined.

4 Spread mixture out in prepared tin, pressing down on mixture with the back of a spoon. Bake for 20 minutes. When it comes out of the oven, press down on it with the back of a spoon again to make it firmer (so it doesn't crumble apart).

5 Leave to cool in the tin then refrigerate for at least 3 hours until firm. Melt chocolate and drizzle over the top, then return to set in the fridge for a further 15 minutes or so before removing and cutting into 8 or 12 bars.

ENERGY	CARBS	PROTEIN	FAT	SAT FAT	SUGARS
845kj / 202kcal	15.1g	5.4g	13g	5.4g	10.4g

Bountiful bars

MAKES 12 bars **PREP TIME** 20 minutes + 1 hour to set in freezer
COOK TIME 5 minutes

DF (use DF dark chocolate) I GF

COCONUT FILLING
coconut cream ¼ cup
maple syrup ¼ cup
coconut oil 4 tablespoons
vanilla essence or extract 1 teaspoon
salt a good pinch
desiccated coconut 3 cups

CHOCOLATE COATING
good-quality milk chocolate
150g, chopped (see Tip page 204)
coconut oil 4 tablespoons
dark cocoa powder (I like to use Dutch
cocoa powder) 1 tablespoon
maple syrup 1½ tablespoons
shredded coconut, to garnish (optional)
lime zest, to garnish (optional)

People go gaga over these Bountiful Bars. Jam-packed with sweet, moist coconut, coated in real chocolate, with a hint of lime zest, these will be a smash hit with any Bounty-bar lover!

1 Place coconut cream and maple syrup in a pot and bring to the boil. Turn off the heat and stir in coconut oil, vanilla and salt until coconut oil has melted; then stir in desiccated coconut until well combined.

2 Spoon mixture into a square 18–20cm baking tin or dish lined with baking or greaseproof paper. Spread out evenly, pressing down with the back of a wet spoon (or with wet hands). Freeze for at least 2 hours, or until solid.

3 Gently melt chopped chocolate and coconut oil together, either in a glass bowl set above a pot of simmering water, in a double boiler or using a microwave. Stir in cocoa and maple syrup until smooth — if the mixture is not runny enough for dipping, add another 1–2 tablespoons melted coconut oil until you get the right consistency. Leave to cool to room temperature on the bench before dipping.

continued over page...

Storage

The bars will last
for 1–2 weeks in
the fridge, or can
be frozen in an
airtight container.

4 Place a wire rack (that will fit in your freezer) on top of a piece of baking paper.

5 Remove coconut filling from tin by lifting out with baking paper. Use a long sharp knife to cut into 12 bars (6 x 2). (Round off the edges with a knife and, if you like, shape with your fingers for a more authentic look.) Carefully dip each bar into melted chocolate, using two forks, to coat completely. Lift out, allow excess chocolate to drip off, then transfer to wire rack.

6 Place bars in the freezer, on the wire rack, for 10 minutes. Remove, then drizzle bars with remaining chocolate (you can run the end of a chopstick through the drizzle to create a ripple pattern if you like). Immediately sprinkle with a little shredded coconut and lime zest (before chocolate hardens), then return to freezer for a further 15 minutes. Then you're free to devour them!

Tips

• You can use dark chocolate instead of milk chocolate for the coating if you prefer, just use 2 tablespoons less of coconut oil.
• To make tropical Bountiful Bars, replace 2 tablespoons maple syrup with 3 tablespoons passionfruit syrup in the coconut filling.

ENERGY	CARBS	PROTEIN	FAT	SAT FAT	SUGARS
1390kj / 332kcal	14.2g	2.8g	28.9g	23.9g	13.9g

Avocado, lime and mint mousse cake

SERVES 8–10 **PREP TIME** 35 minutes + 4–5 hours in fridge **COOK TIME** 10–15 minutes **DF** (use coconut oil) **| GF**

BASE
ground almonds 1 cup
desiccated coconut ¾ cup
medjool dates 8 large, pitted (or 14–16 dried dates, soaked in boiling water for 1 minute, then well drained)
salt good pinch
coconut oil (or melted butter) 5 tablespoons

FILLING
avocados (firm ripe) flesh from 5 medium (remove any brown or stringy bits)
lime juice 1 cup (freshly squeezed or pre-squeezed from a packet)
limes finely grated zest of 1–2
salt good pinch
coconut cream 1 cup
vanilla essence or extract 2 teaspoons
maple syrup 1 cup (or ¾ cup caster sugar)
mint leaves a handful, chopped
gelatine powder 2 tablespoons
cold water 2 tablespoons
boiling water 3 tablespoons

RASPBERRY COULIS
frozen raspberries ¾ cup
honey (or maple syrup or sugar) 1 tablespoon
vanilla essence or extract 1 teaspoon

Storage
The cake (without the coulis) will keep in the fridge for a couple of days, or can be frozen (covered well with clingfilm) for weeks.

This is one of my insanely popular healthier dessert recipes. Believe it or not, avocados are marvellous in desserts (as many of you who've made my avocado chocolate mousse will testify to), lending a rich, creamy texture. Make when good-quality avocados are cheap and abundant, usually in late summer or autumn when their flesh is creamier.

1 Preheat oven to 160°C. Lightly grease and line base and sides of a 20–21cm round spring-form cake tin with baking-paper.

2 Place all base ingredients in a food processor and blitz until well combined and crumbly. The mixture should hold together well when pinched between your fingers. Tip into prepared tin and press mixture down firmly and evenly with the back of a spoon. Bake for 10–15 minutes or until lightly browned, then place in the fridge to cool.

3 To make the filling, place all the ingredients, except the gelatine and water, in a food processor and blend until the mixture is smooth. Taste the mixture and add more maple syrup, lime juice or zest, mint or vanilla, to your liking.

4 Mix gelatine powder with cold water and leave to swell for a few minutes. Add boiling water and mix well to completely dissolve the gelatine (make sure there are no little lumps!). Add gelatine mixture to the food processor and blend with avocado mixture until very smooth and well incorporated.

5 Pour filling over the base. Cover, and return to the fridge to set for at least 4–5 hours or overnight.

6 To make Raspberry Coulis, place raspberries, honey and vanilla in a small pot and boil for a few minutes, mashing up the raspberries. Cool slightly, then blend until smooth, adding a little water until you reach desired consistency.

7 To serve, carefully run a knife between the tin and the cake to loosen before releasing spring latch and removing cake. Drizzle with Raspberry Coulis just before serving.

ENERGY	CARBS	PROTEIN	FAT	SAT FAT	SUGARS
2645kj / 632kcal	38.8g	7.8g	48.7g	18.8g	36.1g

Dreamy passionfruit yoghurt ice-cream terrine

SERVES 6–8 **PREP TIME** 20 minutes + 8 hours in the freezer **COOK TIME** 5 minutes   **GF**

This ice-cream terrine makes a splendid dessert for a dinner party — it looks spectacular with the colourful fruit salsa on top, can be made well in advance and sit in your freezer until you're ready to serve, and people are always impressed by the fact that it's home-made ice-cream! The loaf shape makes it easy to cut and serve this light, refreshing and creamy dessert as slices.

TERRINE
honey (or sugar) ⅔ cup
lemon finely grated zest and juice of 1
free-range egg whites 4, at room temperature
cream ¾ cup
thick Greek yoghurt 1 cup
mango (fresh or frozen and defrosted), diced, 2 cups
passionfruit pulp (from about 4 fresh passionfruit) ⅓ cup
mint tips, a few to garnish

TROPICAL FRUIT SALSA
kiwifruit 2, diced
mango 1, diced
passionfruit pulp of 2
honey (or sugar) 1–2 teaspoons

Tip

Transfer it to the fridge (in the tin) about 15 minutes before you intend to eat it. This will soften it very slightly so it's at the perfect consistency to slice and eat.

1 Line a large loaf tin with clingfilm, with at least 15cm hanging over each side (so that you can wrap the terrine over the top, and it also makes it much easier to remove once frozen).

2 Combine honey, lemon zest and juice in a small pot and bring to the boil. Reduce heat slightly and simmer for about 5 minutes until syrupy (watch carefully that it doesn't boil over).

3 Place egg whites in a large clean, dry metal or glass bowl (not plastic), and beat with an electric beater until stiff peaks form. Reduce beater to low speed and gradually pour in the hot syrup while slowly beating. Increase beater to high speed again and continue beating for about 6–8 minutes or until mixture is thick, glossy and meringue-like.

4 In another large bowl, whip cream to soft peaks, then fold through yoghurt. Add about one-third of the meringue to the yoghurt cream mixture and fold through gently using a large metal spoon (to keep as much air in the mixture as possible) until evenly incorporated. Repeat with remaining meringue.

5 Use a food processor or blender to blend mango until smooth, then mix in passionfruit pulp. Gently swirl/fold through cream mixture. Spoon into prepared tin and smooth the top, making sure there are no air pockets. Cover with overhanging clingfilm and freeze for at least 8 hours or until completely frozen.

6 Mix all salsa ingredients together and set aside.

7 When ready to eat, lift terrine out of the loaf tin (using the overhanging clingfilm to help). Carefully tip terrine onto a serving plate and spoon salsa over the top. Cut into 6–8 slices.

ENERGY	CARBS	PROTEIN	FAT	SAT FAT	SUGARS
1353kj / 323kcal	45g	5.2g	12.9g	7.8g	44g

Black Doris mascarpone ice-cream

SERVES 4 **PREP TIME** 15 minutes + at least 8 hours to freeze plums   **DF** (use coconut yoghurt) | **GF**

Black Doris plums in syrup 2 x 850g cans (reserve ½ cup syrup)
mascarpone 200g (or thick natural yoghurt for a lower-fat version)

Tip

Best eaten within 1–2 days of being frozen. However, it will last a few weeks in the freezer but you will have to let it thaw for about 10 minutes on the bench (or 15 minutes in the fridge) until it becomes easy to scoop again.

This is one of the best ice-cream flavours I've ever had, and my home-made version is even better than the bought version as it's so much more 'plummy' and not overly sweet. I'd say it's halfway between a sorbet and an ice-cream — refreshing and creamy at the same time, with an intense colour and flavour.

1 Cut plums in half and remove stones. Place plums in a dish (or on a tray) lined with baking paper and freeze for at least 8 hours, or overnight, until frozen hard.

2 Place frozen plums (you may need to break them up a little into chunks) in a food processor with mascarpone and blend until completely smooth. Scrape down the sides of the food processor bowl a few times throughout to make sure everything is completely blended. Use a little of the plum syrup to loosen the mixture, if needed.

3 Scoop into a dish or loaf tin, cover and freeze until ready to serve.

	ENERGY	CARBS
	1716kj / 410.5kcal	40.7g

PROTEIN	FAT	SAT FAT	SUGARS
4.0g	6g	2.9g	40.5g

Jelly-tipped ice-creams

RASPBERRY JELLY
frozen raspberries, defrosted, 1½ cups
water ¼ cup
chia seeds 1½ tablespoons
sugar (or maple syrup or liquid honey)
1½ tablespoons

VANILLA ICE-CREAM
cream 1 cup
vanilla bean pod seeds of 1 (or 2
teaspoons vanilla extract with seeds)
sugar 2–3 tablespoons
full-fat thick Greek yoghurt
(or coconut yoghurt) 1 cup

CHOCOLATE SHELL
dark chocolate 100g, chopped
coconut oil 2 tablespoons

Tips

• If you don't have
ice-block moulds, use
small plastic cups and
wooden sticks.
• If using wooden sticks,
semi-freeze Jelly Tipped
Ice-creams for a few
hours before pushing
wooden sticks in so that
they stay put!
• You can make a
dairy-free version by
blending coconut cream
and coconut yoghurt (in
place of cream and
yoghurt), and check dark
chocolate is DF.

*One day I had this brilliant idea on how to make this
nostalgic childhood favourite of mine with no artificial
colours and flavours, just pure, intensely flavoured
raspberry jelly, creamy vanilla ice-cream and a thin crispy
dark chocolate shell made of real dark chocolate. I was
stoked with the result! Biting into one is simply sublime
on a hot summer's day.*

1 To make the raspberry jelly, blend raspberries and water in
a blender for a minute or two until liquid, then push (as
much as you can) through a sieve to remove seeds. Whisk
strained raspberry sauce with chia seeds and sugar and
leave in the fridge for at least 2 hours (in this time the chia
seeds will swell and thicken the raspberry sauce, giving it a
jelly-like texture).

2 To make the Vanilla Ice-cream, whip cream, vanilla and
sugar together until soft peaks form. Fold through yoghurt.

3 Use a spoon to fill 8 ice-block moulds one-third of the way
up with Raspberry Jelly and the remaining two-thirds with
Vanilla Ice-cream, making sure there are no air bubbles.
Freeze for at least 8 hours or overnight.

4 When ice-blocks are frozen, gently melt chocolate and
coconut oil together, stir until well combined and allow to
cool. Remove the ice blocks from the moulds and dip each
side in chocolate (or drizzle chocolate all over). Refreeze for
another 10 minutes or so (in a dish or on a tray lined with
baking paper) until the chocolate shell has hardened.

Storage

Will keep for weeks in the
freezer, just cover them
so they don't take on any
'freezer' smells and tastes.

ENERGY	CARBS	PROTEIN	FAT	SAT FAT	SUGARS
1191kj / 285kcal	15.6g	3.1g	23.1g	14.5g	13.6g

Real vanilla custard

SERVES 4 **PREP TIME** 5 minutes **COOK TIME** 25 minutes   GF

full-fat milk 2 cups (or for a more indulgent, creamier custard replace 1 cup milk with cream)
vanilla bean pod 1 (or 1 teaspoon vanilla essence)
free-range egg yolks 5
sugar (or maple syrup or liquid honey) 3–4 tablespoons

Can be stored in the fridge (covered) for a couple of days.

Real, home-made custard is one of life's most simple and gratifying treats. It sure beats the gluggy shop-bought stuff with its added thickeners. It goes with just about every dessert — served warm to pour over cake, pudding or cooked fruit, or chilled with fresh fruit as a simple dessert. The most important thing when making it, is patience. You really do have to wait by the stovetop, constantly stirring it on low heat. If you don't, you risk ending up with sweet scrambled eggs! Use the leftover egg whites to make my pavlova (page 228) or friands (page 186).

1 Place milk in a small pot. Split vanilla bean pod in half, scrape out seeds and add to milk. Warm milk very gently on low heat — you don't want the milk to be scalding hot, just warm. Do not allow it to come to the boil.

2 In a medium-sized bowl, whisk egg yolks together until smooth. Gradually add warmed milk to bowl of egg yolks, whilst continuously whisking.

3 Tip mixture back into the pot the milk was warmed in and cook on low heat for 20 minutes, while slowly stirring or whisking continuously, until the custard has thickened enough to coat the back of a wooden spoon. Never let the mixture boil or else you risk curdling it! The key is to be patient — it will seem at first as if it's never going to thicken, however, it will, very gradually.

4 Stir in sugar to sweeten to taste. Remove from heat and allow to cool — it will continue to thicken as it cools down.

5 Serve warm or cold with fresh or cooked fruit (e.g. peaches), crumble or just about any dessert that is worthy!

	ENERGY	CARBS
	735kj / 175kcal	16.6g

PROTEIN	FAT	SAT FAT	SUGARS
8.2g	8.3g	2.8g	16.6g

MORE PLEASE.

Indulge and celebrate!

TREATS

MY TOP-TEN FAVOURITE SWEET TREATS FOR SPECIAL OCCASIONS —
BECAUSE LIFE'S TOO SHORT NOT TO ENJOY TREATS EVERY
NOW AND AGAIN!

Tropical coconut cake with whipped white chocolate ganache

SERVES 10–12 **PREP TIME** 40 minutes + 1–2 hours in fridge
COOK TIME 1 hour

GF (use GF flour +1½ teaspoons baking powder)

WHITE CHOCOLATE GANACHE
cream 300ml
white chocolate 125g, chopped

CAKE
butter 100g, softened
coconut oil 50g (or another 50g butter)
caster sugar 1 cup
vanilla essence or extract 2 teaspoons
free-range eggs 4, at room temperature
baking soda 2 level teaspoons
milk (dairy or coconut) ¾ cup, warmed
bananas (very ripe) 2, very well mashed
(to make 1 cup mashed banana)
crushed pineapple 1 cup (from a 425g
can, well drained)
desiccated coconut 1½ cups
self-raising flour 150g, sifted
salt a pinch

TO SERVE
passionfruit syrup ⅓ cup (store-bought
or mix fresh passionfruit pulp with a little
sugar or honey)
coconut chips ¼ cup, lightly toasted
limes zest of 1–2

Tip

You could also make this recipe
as 12 mini cakes, in muffin tins
double lined with paper cases.
Cook for about 30 minutes.

ENERGY		CARBS	
2499kj / 597kcal		48.6g	
PROTEIN	**FAT**	**SAT FAT**	**SUGARS**
7.1g	41.1g	29g	38.6g

*Banana, coconut, pineapple, lime and passionfruit — are you
feeling the vibe? It's an incredibly moist (and obviously fruity)
cake, made extra special with a silky sweet white chocolate
ganache which you whip up to make light and airy. However, a
good cream cheese icing (like the one used for my Watermelon
'Cake' on page 166) would do this cake equal justice.*

1 To make White Chocolate Ganache, gently heat cream in a
bowl in the microwave, or in a pot on the stovetop. Take off
heat, add white chocolate, and stir until melted and a smooth,
silky ganache. Allow to cool in the fridge for at least 1–2 hours
until very cold (do not skip this step!). Once cold, use an
electric beater on high speed to whip up the ganache — it will
take quite a while, at least 5 minutes (longer than it takes to
whip cream by itself). It will seem like it's not going to thicken
much, and then all of a sudden it will — and then you have to
be very careful not to over-whip it or it may become grainy! So
as soon as you see it starting to look like whipped cream, stop
and only continue whipping on very low speed. Place in the
fridge until ready to use.

2 Preheat oven to 160°C. Lightly grease and line base and
sides of a 21–23cm round cake tin with baking paper.

3 In a large mixing bowl, use an electric beater to beat butter,
coconut oil, sugar and vanilla until thick and pale. Beat in eggs,
one at a time, making sure each egg is well incorporated
before adding the next, until mixture is fluffy and creamy.

4 Mix baking soda with warmed milk. Add to creamed mixture
along with mashed banana, pineapple, coconut, flour and salt.
Use a large metal spoon to fold ingredients together until you
have a uniform batter. Spoon into prepared tin and bake for
about 1 hour or until a skewer inserted into the centre comes
out clean. Allow to cool a little then transfer from tin to wire rack.

5 Once cake has cooled, transfer to a plate or cake stand.
Spread ganache over the top and sides of the cake. Garnish
with passionfruit syrup, coconut chips and lime zest.

Easy chocolate cake with stracciatella cream

SERVES 12 **PREP TIME** 25 minutes **COOK TIME** 1 hour

CHOCOLATE CAKE
sugar 1 cup
brown sugar ¾ cup
self-raising flour 1¾ cups
dark cocoa powder (preferably Dutch) ¾ cup
baking soda (lump-free or sifted) 1½ level teaspoons
free-range eggs 3 large, whisked
milk or cream (dairy or coconut) 1 cup
neutral flavoured oil (e.g. grapeseed or a lite olive oil) ¾ cup
salt a good pinch
hot coffee (e.g. instant, filtered, percolator or espresso) ¾ cup

CHOCOLATE GANACHE
cream (dairy or coconut) ⅓ cup
dark chocolate (60–75% cocoa) 100g, chopped
maple syrup (or sugar) 1 tablespoon (optional)

STRACCIATELLA CREAM
cream cheese 200g, softened
lemon juice 1–2 tablespoons
lemon finely grated zest of 1
vanilla essence or extract 1 teaspoon
cream 300ml
icing sugar 3 tablespoons
dark chocolate, 75–100g, finely chopped

I can quite easily pass on chocolate cake most of the time. But don't fret (seeing this is a chocolate cake recipe!), it just means I have higher expectations when it comes to chocolate cake and only deem a really moist, sumptuous chocolate cake worth eating. This cake is that, plus it's dead easy to make — the cake itself is only one 'mix and bake' step!

1 Preheat oven to 170°C. Lightly grease and line the base and sides of a 20-21cm round cake tin with baking paper.

2 Place all chocolate cake ingredients, except coffee, into a large mixing bowl and mix together well with a fork, then pour in coffee and continue mixing until a smooth batter. Pour into prepared cake tin and bake for about 1 hour or until a skewer inserted into the centre of the cake comes out clean.

3 Allow cake to cool in the tin before removing and transferring onto a wire cake rack. Leave to cool completely before filling and icing.

4 To make the Chocolate Ganache, heat cream in microwave or on the stovetop to almost a boil (but do not let it boil). Stir in chocolate until ganache is smooth and silky. Stir in maple syrup (if using). Leave to cool (it will thicken as it cools).

5 To make the Stracciatella Cream, use an electric beater to beat cream cheese, lemon juice, zest and vanilla together in a large bowl, until smooth. Add cream and icing sugar and continue beating for 2–3 minutes until it is like very thick whipped cream — be careful not to overbeat or you may risk it splitting. Fold in chopped chocolate and chill until ready to use.

6 When cake has completely cooled, carefully cut in half horizontally using a large serrated knife. Spread Stracciatella Cream all over bottom layer, then add top layer. Once Chocolate Ganache has cooled, spread over the top and sides of the cake.

ENERGY	CARBS		
2603kj / 622kcal	52.8g		
PROTEIN	**FAT**	**SAT FAT**	**SUGARS**
7.9g	42g	17.3g	36.5g

Little lemon butterfly cakes

MAKES 12 **PREP TIME** 15 minutes **COOK TIME** 20–25 minutes

These beautiful little cakes will make your heart flutter. They're super light and lemony, and such a delight for any special occasion.

caster sugar ¾ cup
butter 200g, softened
vanilla essence or extract 1 teaspoon
free-range eggs 4, at room temperature
salt a pinch
lemons zest of 2
self-raising flour 200g

TOPPING
lemons juice of 1½
sugar 3 tablespoons
lemon or passionfruit curd
(shop-bought or home-made, page 237)
or Raspberry Chia Jam (see page 20)
cream ½ cup, whipped
icing sugar, to dust

1 Preheat oven to 170°C. Line a 12-hole muffin tin with paper cups.

2 In a large bowl, beat (either with an electric beater or a wooden spoon and lots of elbow grease) sugar, butter and vanilla until thick, pale and creamy.

3 Beat in eggs, one at a time, making sure each egg is well incorporated after each addition.

4 Add salt and lemon zest, and sift in flour. Stir until just combined.

5 Spoon mixture into paper cases, dividing equally. Bake for about 25 minutes or until risen, light golden and the cakes spring back when very gently pressed in the middle.

6 To make the topping, mix lemon juice and sugar together and drizzle over the cakes while still warm in the tin. Leave to cool in the tin for 10 minutes before moving to a wire rack to cool completely.

7 To make into butterfly cakes, simply slice a little off the top of each cake and cut slice in half. Top each cake with curd or jam and a dollop of whipped cream, then arrange 'wings' on top and dust with icing sugar.

ENERGY	CARBS	PROTEIN	FAT	SAT FAT	SUGARS
1339kj / 320kcal	31.8g	4.3g	19.7g	12.1g	20.5g

Wicked coffee, toffee and walnut slice

MAKES 25 pieces **PREP TIME** 15 minutes
COOK TIME 40 minutes + 2–3 hours in the fridge

GF (use ground almonds)

There's one word to describe this slice: wicked. Having it in the house is a hazard as you will keep going back to slice off a little more every time you pass the kitchen bench. Personally, I have to plan who I'm going to give it to before I bake it because I don't have the willpower to only have one piece. It is, without a doubt, one of the best caramel slices you will ever eat. The coffee part is optional.

BASE
fine (quick cook) rolled oats ¾ cup (or ground almonds)
desiccated or shredded coconut 1¼ cup
medjool dates (or dried figs) 6, pitted (or 10 normal dried dates soaked in hot water for 5 minutes, then well drained)
salt a pinch
melted butter (or coconut oil) 6 tablespoons

TOPPING
butter 120g, cubed
golden syrup ⅓ cup
sweetened condensed milk 2x 395g cans
instant coffee granules 3–4 teaspoons, dissolved in 2 tablespoons boiling water (optional)
walnuts, roughly chopped, 1 cup

1 Preheat oven to 180°C. Line the base and sides of a 20cm square baking tin with baking paper.

2 Place oats, coconut, dates, salt and butter in a food processor (or see Tip) and blitz until well combined and the mixture holds together when you pinch it between your fingers. If it doesn't hold together, you may need to add a little more butter. Press mixture into lined baking tin, pressing down firmly with the back of a wet spoon or spatula. Bake for 10 minutes while you make the topping.

3 To make the topping, place butter and golden syrup in a pot and stir over low heat until the butter has melted and everything is smooth and combined. Take off the heat and stir in condensed milk and coffee (if using) until smooth.

4 Pour caramel over the base and scatter walnuts on top. Bake for a further 30 minutes until golden and a little bubbly. Refrigerate for at least a few hours until cold, then slice into 25 squares.

Tips

• If you don't have a food processor, boil dates with a splash of water, stirring often, until a mushy paste. Then mix with remaining base ingredients.
• It helps to use a hot, wet, sharp knife to cut the slice.
• To make a chocolate caramel slice, replace the walnuts with a chocolate icing made by beating butter with icing sugar and dark cocoa powder (or a mixture of melted chocolate and butter).

ENERGY	CARBS	PROTEIN	FAT	SAT FAT	SUGARS
1085kj / 260kcal	24.9g	4.9g	15.5g	9g	23.3g

Incredibly rich dark chocolate mud cake

SERVES 10–12 **PREP TIME** 15 minutes **COOK TIME** 35 minutes **DF** (use coconut oil instead of butter + check chocolate) **| GF**

good-quality dark chocolate (I used Whittaker's 72% Dark Ghana) 350g
butter 250g
free-range eggs 5
brown sugar ½ cup

This cake is simply epic: four simple ingredients result in the most intense, rich, unctuous chocolate cake, almost like baked chocolate mousse. When it comes out of the oven you want the middle to still be wobbly and moist, sticky even; this will allow for that gorgeous fudgy (or mud-like) texture in the middle.

1 Preheat oven to 170°C. Line the base and sides of a 20–21cm round spring-form cake tin with baking paper.

2 Gently melt chocolate and butter together, either in the microwave or on the stovetop, stirring a few times, until completely melted. Set aside to cool to room temperature.

3 While chocolate is cooling, place eggs and brown sugar in a large mixing bowl and beat with an electric beater, on high speed, for 4–5 minutes or until mixture is very fluffy and pale, and about 4–5 times larger in volume.

4 Use a large metal spoon to fold melted chocolate into egg mixture until chocolate is uniformly mixed through. Try to keep as much air in the batter as possible. Spoon mixture into prepared cake tin and bake for 30–35 minutes until the top has formed a thin crust, has a very slight wobble in the middle, and a skewer inserted into the centre comes out with a few slightly sticky crumbs. (Note: the cake will have puffed up and sunken back in a little, which is to be expected).

5 Allow to cool for at least 10 minutes before removing cake from tin. Serve warm or at room temperature by itself or with yoghurt, cream or ice-cream, and maybe some raspberries or strawberries to balance out the richness.

ENERGY	CARBS	PROTEIN	FAT	SAT FAT	SUGARS
1687kj / 403kcal	17.8g	5.6g	34.3g	20.8g	14.4g

Brown sugar pavlova with salted caramel, pear and hazelnuts

SERVES 8–10 **PREP TIME** 40–45 minutes **COOK TIME** 1 hour 15 minutes + at least 2 hours to cool **GF**

BROWN SUGAR PAVLOVA
free-range egg whites 6 large,
at room temperature
caster sugar 1 cup
soft brown sugar ¾ cup
white vinegar 1 teaspoon
cornflour 4 teaspoons

POACHED PEARS
star anise 3–4
cinnamon sticks 2
white wine (or water or apple/orange
juice) 1 cup
water 3 cups
lemon peeled skin (cut into thin strips)
and juice of 1
soft brown sugar ⅓ cup
white sugar ⅓ cup
pears (just ripe) 6 small firm (e.g. Honey
belle, Beurre bosc)

SALTED CARAMEL SAUCE
butter 45g (3 tablespoons)
golden syrup 2 tablespoons
brown sugar ¼ cup
cream 2 tablespoons
flaky sea salt ⅛ teaspoon

CINNAMON YOGHURT CREAM
cream 1 cup
**natural unsweetened thick Greek
   yoghurt** (or coconut yoghurt) ½ cup
ground cinnamon 1½ teaspoons
vanilla essence or extract 1 teaspoon
icing sugar 2 tablespoons

TO GARNISH
roasted hazelnuts, chopped, about
⅓ cup
dark chocolate, chopped, about ¼ cup

This pav is a thing of beauty! Salted caramel, pear and hazelnuts are one killer of a flavour combination, atop pillows of cinnamon-spiked cream and a crisp chewy meringue base, with hints of caramel (the result of using brown sugar in the meringue). Perfect for the Christmas table or any special occasion. Use the leftover yolks to make my Real Vanilla Custard (page 214) or Your One and Only Crème Brûlée (page 240).

1 To make the pavlova, preheat oven to 160°C. Line a baking tray with baking paper, and mark an 18–20cm circle on it using a plate as a stencil. Sieve over a little cornflour (this helps prevent the pavlova from sticking).

2 Place egg whites in a large, clean, dry stainless steel or glass bowl. Use an electric beater to whip until foamy, then gradually add caster sugar and brown sugar, whilst continuing to whip for about 8 minutes on high speed, until all the sugar is dissolved and it is thick and glossy. Quickly fold through vinegar and cornflour. Spoon pavlova mixture into the circle on the baking paper, making sure the base is covered well. If you like, you can smooth the mixture out to create a flat surface, but I prefer to leave it in dollops and swirls.

3 Bake for 1 hour 15 minutes. Turn off oven and leave pavlova to cool in the oven completely without opening the oven door. Don't worry if the pavlova has a few cracks in it — this is a good sign that it's got a crispy shell and marshmallowy inside, and it will be covered in cream anyway!

4 To make the Poached Pears, mix all ingredients, except pears, in a medium-sized pot. Peel pears as nicely and smoothly as you can with a vegetable peeler. Place pears in the wine mixture on their side so that they are covered by the liquid. Bring to a gentle boil, then reduce heat and simmer gently, partially covered, for 1½–2 hours, or until

continued over page...

pears are tender, and the liquid has reduced to a golden amber-coloured syrup. Baste pears with the syrup a few times during cooking and check that the liquid is not reducing so quickly that the pears start burning on the bottom of the pot. Turn the pears over at least once during cooking so that both sides have a turn being fully submerged in the liquid.

5 To make the Salted Caramel Sauce, heat butter, golden syrup and brown sugar in a pot on medium heat. Simmer for about 2 minutes, then remove from the heat and stir in cream and salt to taste. Set aside to cool.

6 To make the Cinnamon Yoghurt Cream, whip cream then fold in remaining ingredients.

7 To assemble, slice poached pears. Smother pavlova with Cinnamon Yoghurt Cream, top with pears, drizzle with Salted Caramel Sauce and scatter with hazelnuts and chocolate. If you like, drizzle some of the poached pear syrup on top too.

Tips

• It may sound strange, but older eggs are best for making meringue — the whites whip up much better than those of very fresh eggs.
• The Poached Pears can be made in advance and stored in the fridge (in their syrup) for up to a week.
• The pavlova can be made in advance and stored in a large airtight container for up to a few days.
• The Cinnamon Yoghurt Cream can be made a day before and stored, well covered, in the fridge until ready to assemble.
• The Salted Caramel Sauce can be made up to a few days in advance and stored in the fridge.

PERFECT PAVLOVA

ENERGY	CARBS	PROTEIN	FAT	SAT FAT	SUGARS
2336kj / 559kcal	73.9g	6.1g	23.6g	12.9g	72.1g

Black Forest Eton mess

SERVES 4 PREP TIME 30 minutes COOK TIME 15 minutes   GF

dark fleshed cherries (fresh or frozen)
500–600g, pitted
sugar 3 tablespoons
lemon juice of ½
water 2 tablespoons
kirsch or brandy 3–4 tablespoons
cream 1½ cups
vanilla bean pod seeds of 1
dark chocolate 100g, chopped
meringues 8 small

Ripples of boozy cherry compôte, a layer of crushed meringue, lashings of vanilla cream and swirls of melted dark chocolate make this Christmas-time favourite one hell of a sumptuous dessert. It's also easy to make, with all components able to be made in advance.

1 Place cherries, sugar, lemon juice and water in a pot on medium heat. Cook, stirring frequently, for about 15 minutes or until fruit is soft, a deep colour and liquid is syrupy. Stir in kirsch or brandy and allow to cool completely.

2 Whip cream and vanilla to soft peaks.

3 Melt chocolate either in a glass bowl set above a pot of barely simmering water or in a double boiler, or in the microwave. Set aside to cool at room temperature.

4 Roughly crumble the meringues and divide between serving glasses. Top with half the cream and half the cherries and syrup, dividing equally. Repeat layers, drizzle over chocolate, then serve immediately. Alternatively, just before serving, gently fold cherries and chocolate through the cream (fold no more than 2–3 times so you get a beautiful swirl effect) and layer this on top of crushed meringue in glasses.

Tip

You can use the base of a chopstick to push the stones out of the cherries instead of using a cherry pitter (because who has one of those?!).

ENERGY	CARBS	PROTEIN	FAT	SAT FAT	SUGARS
2995kj / 716kcal	58.2g	6.1g	48.5g	29.6g	55.4g

Luscious lemon cheesecake

SERVES 8–10 **PREP TIME** 20 minutes + 3 hours in the fridge **COOK TIME** 1 hour

LEMON CURD
free-range egg yolks 4
caster sugar ½ cup
lemon juice (freshly squeezed) ½ cup

BASE
gingernut or wine biscuits 125g (half a packet)
dried dates ⅓ cup
butter 50g, melted
salt a pinch

FILLING
sour cream 250g
cream cheese 400g, softened
caster sugar ⅓ cup
vanilla bean pod seeds of 1 (or 2 teaspoons vanilla extract or essence)
lemons finely grated zest of 2
free-range eggs 3, at room temperature
lemon curd ½ cup, home-made (see recipe above) or shop-bought (but make sure it's a good quality one)

This baked cheesecake is simply irresistible. It's gloriously rippled with sweet, sharp lemon curd to bring the perfect balance to the creamy filling and gingernut base. Home-made lemon curd is so much better than shop-bought. There are some good ones you can buy from artisan producers, but it is well worth making your own.

1 Preheat oven to 150°C. Lightly grease and line the base and sides of a 20–21cm round spring-form cake tin with baking paper.

2 If you are making your own Lemon Curd, whisk egg yolks with caster sugar in a medium-sized glass or metal bowl, until well combined. Whisk in lemon juice. Sit bowl above a pot of gently simmering water (or use a double boiler) and gently stir or whisk continuously until mixture is a sauce consistency and has thickened enough to lightly coat the back of a wooden spoon, about 10 minutes. Set aside in the fridge to cool before using (it will thicken as it cools).

3 Put all base ingredients in the food processor (or see Tip) and blitz until a fine crumb and the mixture holds together when pinched between your fingers. You may need to scrape down the sides of the food processor once or twice to make sure everything gets blitzed.

4 Tip base mixture into prepared tin and press down firmly and evenly with the back of a large spoon.

5 Put all filling ingredients, except lemon curd, in food processor and blend until smooth.

continued over page...

6 Pour mixture over the base. Dollop lemon curd over cheesecake, then use a teaspoon to create a swirly pattern. (If using shop-bought lemon curd, which tends to be thicker than home-made, mix it with a teaspoon or two of lemon juice to loosen it.)

7 Bake for 1 hour or until cheesecake is just set (if you give it a gentle jiggle it should still have a bit of a wobble in the middle). Remove from oven and allow to cool for 10–15 minutes before placing in fridge to chill and set for at least 3 hours, before removing from tin and serving.

Tips

• If you don't have a food processor, you can break and smash up the biscuits in a plastic bag with a rolling pin until they become fine crumbs. Cook dates with a splash of water in a small pot, stirring frequently until a mushy paste. Then mix with the biscuit crumbs and remaining base ingredients. And for the filling, use an electric beater to beat cream cheese in a large bowl until smooth, then beat in sour cream, sugar, vanilla and lemon zest, then eggs, one at a time, until well incorporated.
• Turn it into a lemon passionfruit cheesecake by adding the pulp of 4 ripe passionfruit to the curd before swirling it through.

Storage

This cheesecake will last in the fridge, covered, for up to 5 days.

ENERGY	CARBS	PROTEIN
2015kj / 482kcal	41.2g	6.7g

FAT	SAT FAT	SUGARS
32.3g	18.7g	35.5g

Your one and only crème brûlée

SERVES 6 **PREP TIME** 15 minutes + 3 hours or more in the fridge **COOK TIME** 1 hour GF

You'd think this classic dessert would involve complicated technique, but it's surprisingly simple to make — well, with this foolproof recipe anyway! It's the one and only crème brûlée recipe you'll ever need (you can add all kinds of flavours using the basic recipe). I've made it countless times for a dinner party dessert and it never fails me, or fails to impress. With the leftover egg whites you can make my Brown Sugar Pavlova with Poached Pears, Salted Caramel and Hazelnuts (page 228).

BASIC VANILLA CRÈME BRÛLÉE
free-range egg yolks 6
vanilla bean pod seeds of 1 (or 1 teaspoon vanilla extract)
caster sugar 2 tablespoons + 2 tablespoons extra for topping
cream 600ml

1 Preheat oven to 150°C. In a mixing bowl, use a whisk to whisk egg yolks, vanilla and sugar together until pale and the sugar is dissolved.

2 Slowly pour cream into the egg mixture, gently whisking continuously. Pour custard into a jug (this will make pouring into ramekins easier) and pour evenly into six ramekins.

3 Place ramekins in a large baking dish and pour in enough hot water (from the tap is fine) to come halfway up the sides of the ramekins. Carefully transfer to oven and cook for 50–60 minutes until they are just set, with a slight wobble in the middle. Allow to cool slightly, then refrigerate for at least a few hours to set (or in the freezer for about 30 minutes).

4 When ready to serve, evenly sprinkle one teaspoon of sugar over each brûlée. Use a cook's blowtorch to caramelise the sugar. The caramel will harden after about 1 minute. If you don't have a blowtorch, allow crème brûlée to set in the fridge for at least 8 hours (or overnight) until they are very set and cold, then sprinkle over sugar and place under a hot grill (with the oven door open) for 1 minute to caramelise the sugar. Watch like a hawk!

Chocolate crème brûlée

In a pot, heat the **cream** with 75g chopped dark (at least 70% cocoa) **chocolate** until almost a boil (but do not let boil). Take off the heat and whisk until smooth and chocolate is fully incorporated (there should be no brown specs of chocolate left), allow to cool, then follow recipe above.

Raspberry passionfruit crème brûlée

Before cooking, top each crème brûlée with 3 fresh **raspberries** and drizzle with 1 teaspoon **passionfruit syrup**.

	ENERGY	CARBS	PROTEIN	FAT	SAT FAT	SUGARS
Vanilla	1961kj / 469kcal	12.1g	4.9g	45.1g	26.3g	12.1g
Chocolate	2258kj / 540kcal	16.4g	5.8g	50.5g	29.3g	15.1g
Berry	1967kj / 471kcal	12.3g	4.9g	45.1g	26.3g	12.3g

Cassata ice-cream bombe Alaskas

CASSATA ICE-CREAM
plain or French vanilla ice-cream 1 litre
currants 2 tablespoons
brandy (or rum, whisky, amaretto or
other liqueur) ¼ cup
square sponge cake 1 (shop-bought or
homemade, for a gluten-free version see
Coconut Flour Sponge Cake on page
160) or panettone
cherry, raspberry or strawberry jam
1½ tablespoons
water 1–2 teaspoons
lemon zest of 1
fresh or frozen raspberries ¾ cup
fresh or frozen mixed berries
(e.g. strawberries, blackberries,
boysenberries, blueberries,
blackcurrants) ½ cup
pistachios, chopped, ¼ cup
almonds, chopped, ¼ cup
almond essence ½ teaspoon (optional)

MERINGUE TOPPING
free-range egg whites 3 large
caster sugar ¾ cup

TO SERVE
brandy (or whisky) 4–6 tablespoons,
heated

*This dessert is guaranteed to get squeals of delight —
especially when you set it alight! Sweet fluffy meringue
encases Cassata (ice-cream flavoured with berries, dried fruit,
lemon and nuts (and booze). It may sound daunting, but it's
much easier than you think — I've 'cheated' a little to make it
quicker and easier by just using shop-bought ice-cream. You
could cheat even more and just use shop-bought sponge too!*

1 Get ice-cream out of the freezer and leave on the bench to
thaw and soften for about 10 minutes while you get on with
the rest. Combine currants and brandy in a bowl and leave to
soak for at least 10–15 minutes.

2 Line six 1-cup capacity ramekins, teacups or little bowls with
clingfilm, with enough excess to hang over the sides by about
6cm (that you can use to cover the bombes, and it also makes
it easier to lift out of the moulds afterwards).

3 Using an upside-down mould and a knife, cut 3 circles out of
the sponge. Cut each in half horizontally, so you have 6
rounds, each approximately 1cm thick. Loosen jam with water,
then spread over sponge. Set aside.

4 Drain currants, reserving the liquid. Scoop ice-cream into a
large mixing bowl and work it with a wooden spoon to soften
enough so that you can mix it with other ingredients (but do
not allow ice-cream to thaw completely). Working quickly,
roughly mix in soaked currants, lemon zest, berries, nuts and
almond essence (if using).

continued over page...

5 Spoon ice-cream into lined moulds, pressing down firmly after every few spoonfuls to make sure there are no air gaps. Top each with a round of sponge (jam-side down). Press down firmly on top to completely cover ice-cream, making sure there are no gaps. Drizzle reserved currant soaking liquid over the sponge. Wrap over excess cling film and freeze for at least 8–10 hours, overnight, or longer until it is frozen very hard. You can keep these in the freezer for up to 2 months.

6 Fifteen minutes before serving the bombes, preheat oven to 200°C and line a baking tray with baking paper. To make the Meringue Topping, place egg whites in a clean, dry (stainless steel or glass) bowl and whip with an electric beater on high speed until foamy. Gradually add caster sugar, continuing to whip on high speed for about 5 minutes, until you have a thick, glossy meringue.

7 Take bombes out of freezer and lift out of the moulds using excess clingfilm. Invert onto prepared baking tray, remove clingfilm and, working quickly, spread each bombe with meringue to completely cover (make sure there are no gaps and that the meringue covers the bombes right to the bottom). Bake for 5–6 minutes, switching to grill for the last 2 minutes, or until very lightly browned. Use a fish slice to carefully transfer bombes to serving plates.

8 Pour hot brandy into a heatproof jug (a metal milk jug or Pyrex jug), use a match to ignite it, then pour over the bombes and watch them set alight at the table!

Tips

• You need to use a liquor that is at least 40 percent alcohol for it to set alight. Heat the alcohol by microwaving it for about 45 seconds or in a small pot on the stovetop. Use a heatproof jug for the liquor as it can get hot when you set it alight.
• Darken the room when you set the bombes alight so you can see the flames!

Storage

You can keep the bombes (without meringue) in the freezer for up to two months.

ENERGY	CARBS	PROTEIN	FAT	SAT FAT	SUGARS
2200kj / 526kcal	68.8g	8.8g	20.2g	9.3g	68.1g

THANK YOU

Like a dessert that's so good its taste lingers and lives on way past the moment it's been gobbled up, the bonds made through working together on a project like this book will live on way past the completion of it.

THANK YOU...

Todd for the 'I want to eat the page' photography, and being Mr. Cool 'n Calm — love working with you. **Tanya** for the A-MA-ZING book design, you are one clever cookie, and all-round cool lady! **Lauren** for the gorgeous prop styling and being Ms Fun (and a little crazy) on shoots! **Annabel** for being my 2IC chief taste tester after Carlos and Bodhi, and another foodie brain to banter with. **Ellie** for happily helping out with lots of bits and bobs. **Bella** for being a whizz with the nutrition analyses. **Jane** for your speedy, faultless editing. **Tracey** and **Bryce** for your help and guidance with this project. **Sam** for the very cool title typography. My besties **Rosy**, **Dubby**, **Brendon** and **Guillaume** for being long-time taste testers, critics, supporters and laugh-makers (love you guys to bits) and also being model 'cookbook models'. And also 'Cam-ily', 'Jen-sco' and 'Mc-Binney' who didn't make it onto the pages of this book but hopefully will in the next! Sam, Harry, Kellie-Anne, Sophie, Rachel, Scarlett and Zoe for being such good eaters and cookbook models. My mum and number-one fan, my little sis and bro, and a HUGE thanks to Carlos for putting up with the house being turned upside-down while making this book, and Bodhi for being good for mummy (most of the time).

Most importantly, thank **YOU**, my 'fans' (or as I prefer to call you, my 'foodie friends') from my online community and all corners of New Zealand and other parts of the world. Without you I wouldn't have the opportunity to make this book and do what I love doing. With all your cooking, you're making the world happier and healthier — and I thank you for that.

Thank you also to Artedomus, Junk & Disorderly, Farmers, Citta Design, Alex & Corban, Nest, Freedom Furniture, Republic Home, The Homestore, Yvonne Sanders Antiques and Martha's Fabrics for the hire of your gorgeous props.

INDEX

Text © Nude Food Inc, 2017
Photographs © Todd Eyre, 2017
Typographical design © Nude Food Inc, 2017

Published in 2017 by Nude Food Inc, Auckland, New Zealand

www.nadialim.com

ISBN 978-0-47340-018-7

Book design: Tanya Wong
Illustrations: Tanya Wong
Styling: Lauren Freeman
Edited by: Jane Hingston
Production management: Tracey Borgfeldt

Printed in China through Colorcraft Ltd, Hong Kong